ETYMOLOGICAL INJUSTICE

YOUTH, INCARCERATION, AND SOCIETAL REINTEGRATION

WOODGER FAUGAS

CITADEL PRESS
ACADEMIC PUBLISHING

Published in the United States, by Citadel Press Academic Publishing.

Faugas, Woodger
Etymological Injustice

Hardcover ISBN	979-8-9875566-0-3
E-book ISBN	979-8-9875566-1-0
Paperback ISBN	979-8-9875566-3-4
DOI	10.6084/m9.figshare.23272838

https://doi.org/10.6084/m9.figshare.23272838

https://bookmetahub.scienceopen.com/hosted-document?doi=10.6084/m9.figshare.23272838

PRINTED IN THE UNITED STATES OF AMERICA

First Edition: May 2023

To Amy Faugas,
my *poto mitan*,
and 2012 National Geographic Traveler of the Year,
whose more than 5,000 walked miles across Africa,
I could never match.

This page left blank intentionally

ETYMOLOGICAL INJUSTICE

YOUTH, INCARCERATION, AND SOCIETAL REINTEGRATION

W O O D G E R F A U G A S

This page left blank intentionally

PREFACE

This book has a specific audience: people who think highly of racial justice and human rights but who, for untold reasons, do not yet grasp the depth and seriousness of the obstacles facing youth with sociophysiological challenges, particularly those who have been incarcerated. I took years to write this book for all those whose health and socio-economic needs have been relegated to the margins of American society because of their limitations. Others may have attempted to leave you behind but I, and other advocates, have not forgotten you.

In the pages that follow, this book attempts to refute the idea that it is impossible for youth who were formerly-incarcerated to succeed. Despite the fact that these young people with special needs may struggle with their efforts to re-adapt after periods of incarceration, the challenges they face can be overcome with bolstered and suitable direction. It is thus critical to encourage early intervention where instruction and support services are aimed at bolstering existing abilities and providing necessary resources. Parents, guardians, and educators should consistently acknowledge and celebrate the progress these young people make, no matter how small, as they journey towards more signi icant achievements. Numerous young people with special needs are successfully navigating life and achieving independence.

This page left blank intentionally

CONTENTS

This page left blank intentionally

This page left blank intentionally

CHAPTER I

INTRODUCTION

"There can be no keener revelation of a society's soul than the way it treats its children." (Pretoria, May 1995).[1]

Nelson Mandela,
Former President of South Africa

Two years after entering the Oval Office, former United States (U.S.) President Barack Obama wrote the preface to *Conversations with Myself*, a collected-works paperback woven out of former South Africa President Nelson Mandela's writings and speeches. In this segment of *Conversations*, Obama writes how he had only known of Mandela, affectionately called Madiba, "from a distance"[2] —although the two had already met, when Obama held

[1] Stanley, Fiona. "From Susser's causal paradigms to social justice in Australia?." *International journal of epidemiology* 31, no. 1 (2002): 40-45.

[2] Mandela, Nelson. *Conversations with myself*. Anchor Canada, 2011.

office as a U.S. Senator.

Regarding Madiba's protracted stint in a prison in apartheid South Africa, Obama mentions that it was a "sacrifice...*so great* (emphasis mine) that it called upon people everywhere to do what they could on behalf of human progress."[3] Obama elaborates how, "In the modest of ways," he embraced Madiba's call to sacrifice and became politically active as a community organizer.[4]

To humbly emulate Obama's move, although in a vein that is largely academic, I tackle, in this book, incarceration and the experiences of young people who have dealt with it. Drawing on the connections between societal structures and my past involvements —with people with sociophysiological challenges, at an advocacy organization named Access Living and African-American young men

[3] *Ibid.*, p. 11.

[4] At age 44, Nelson Mandela's peno-judicial foray, or journey across South Africa's prison and court systems, began. He arrived on Robben Island when it was a penal complex situated on an oval landmass west of the coast of Cape Town, South Africa. Mandela spent 18 of his 27 years of imprisonment on the Island, with no bed and a bucket as his urinal and toilet. Despite its toll, prison became the crucible that transformed Mandela into the celebrated figure he later became. The would-be South African president emerged from Robben Island an exemplary leader who would take on the daunting political battles that birthed a democratic South Africa. Years after leaving prison, in *The Long Walk to Freedom* autobiography, Mandela remarked on his time in prison that "... isolation became a habit" and "The authorities believed that isolation was the cure for our defiance and rebelliousness." Mandela, Nelson Rolihlahla. *Long walk to freedom: The autobiography of Nelson Mandela.* No. 92 M271-l. London, GB: Abacus, 1995: 65. In 1993, in Oslo, Norway, while voicing, at the Nobel Peace Prize Ceremony, his gratitude and thoughts on some issues that he considered salient at the time, Mandela declared that "Children are the most vulnerable citizens in any society and the greatest of our treasures." Stanley, *supra* note 1. Having drawn its inspiration from Obama's example, this work inherits its thematic focus from Mandela, whose 1993 speech made children as one of its foci.

and women, as an Albert Schweitzer fellow —I take issue with an important set of issues. To date, incarceration officials have made little to no progress among the various imbalances haunting the juvenile delinquency system. Young people with sociophysiological challenges and are of African-American origin remain vulnerable to being trapped in the maelstrom that is the white–owned and –managed so-called "juvenile justice" system.

This page left blank intentionally

CHAPTER II

METHODOLOGY

A. Thesis Statement

This work aims to support a two-front position: (1) that the U.S. is not doing enough to meet the needs of youth who have been incarcerated and are looking to better their lives after confinement; and (2) that U.S. policymakers need to adopt and implement a number of solution-oriented measures and legal reforms in order to position youth for becoming productive adult members of society.

B. Problem Statement

i. Numerical Scope of the Youth Affected

At issue are problems facing two camps of young people, aged 10 to 24:[5] those of all races with sociophysiological challenges and those who

[5] This age range is based on the age spectrum set by Part B of the Individuals with Disabilities Education Act (IDEA), which provides eligible children with disabilities, aged between 3 and 21, with the right to a free appropriate public education (FAPE).

are African-American. The problems that are of concern relate to the drawbacks of incarceration and the barriers facing youth when attempting to reintegrate in society after serving time for serious crimes and status offenses. These offenses are a class of noncriminal mischiefs, comprising but not limited to truancy, underage drinking, disruptive behavior, and other legal transgressions that apply solely to minors.[6]

The downsides of incarceration, such as diminished income in contrast to never-incarcerated peers, and the upsides of community re-entry, such as avoidance of recidivism, are issues that merit research because they affect a large number of lives. According to the latest U.S. Census Bureau data available, as of 2015, there were roughly 105 million young people, age-24-and-under, in the United States, representing about a third (33%) of Americans.[7] Of these 24-and-under youth, 64,470,546, or about 61.5%, fall within the above-mentioned 10 to 24 age group.[8] Of the 64.47 million youth, between 4 to 5.2 percent, or 2.5 to 3.3 million, of all races have a sociophysiological challenge. In contrast, about 16%, or 9 million, of the total number of

---

[6] Rankin, Joseph H., and L. Edward Wells. "From status to delinquent offenses: Escalation?." *Journal of Criminal Justice* 13, no. 2 (1985): 171-180.

[7] U.S. Census Bureau. "Annual Estimates of the Resident Population for Selected Age Groups by Sex for the United States, States, Counties, and Puerto Rico Commonwealth and Municipios: April 1, 2010 to July 1, 2015." Population Division, 2015. Accessed May 10, 2017. https://factfinder.census.gov/faces/tableservices/jsf/pages/productview.xhtml?src=bkmk.

[8] *Ibid.*

youth are African-American.[9]

Based on conclusions drawn from the latest year of data that Child Trends, an organization aiming to improve youth's lives and prospects, publishes: 410,900 young people were in jail or prison in 2010.[10] Of the youth in jail or prison, as many as 70% have a sociophysiological challenge.[11] In terms of racial make-up, an unbalanced share of African-Africans, at least 31%, comprise all arrests.[12] This difference extends to juveniles who face referrals to juvenile courts, leading to more African-Americans coping with the direct and indirect

---

[9] U.S. Census Bureau. "Annual Estimates of the Resident Population by Sex, Age, Race, and Hispanic Origin for the United States and States: April 1, 2010 to July 1, 2015" Population Division, 2015. Accessed May 10, 2017. https://factfinder.census.gov/faces/tableservices/jsf/pages/productview.xhtml?src=bkmk.

[10] Child Trends. *Young Adults in Jail or in Prison: Indicators of Child and Youth Well-Being*. Child Trends Data Bank, 2012. Accessed May 10, 2017. https://www.childtrends.org/wp-content/uploads/2012/04/89_Young_Adults_In_Prison-1.pdf.

[11] Quinn, Mary Magee, Robert B. Rutherford, Peter E. Leone, David M. Osher, and Jeffrey M. Poirier. "Youth with disabilities in juvenile corrections: A national survey." *Exceptional children* 71, no. 3 (2005): 339-345 *quoting* Casey, Pamela, and Ingo Keilitz. "Estimating the prevalence of learning disabled and mentally retarded juvenile offenders: A meta-analysis." *Understanding troubled and troubling youth* (1990): 82-101; Murphy, Donna M. "The prevalence of handicapping conditions among juvenile delinquents." *Remedial and Special Education* 7, no. 3 (1986): 7-17; Rutherford Jr, Robert B., C. Michael Nelson, and Bruce I. Wolford. "Special education in the most restrictive environment: Correctional/special education." *The Journal of Special Education* 19, no. 1 (1985): 59-71.

[12] The Sentencing Project. *Disproportionate Minority Contact in the Juvenile Justice System*. Policy Brief, 2015. Accessed May 10, 2017. http://www.sentencingproject.org/wp-content/uploads/2015/11/Disproportionate-Minority-Contact-in-the-Juvenile-Justice-System.pdf.

effects of incarceration.

ii. Problem's Importance

Youth incarceration and reintegration deserve attention because if our society fails youth with sociophysiological challenges and those who are African American, by denying them a chance at self-redemption, we risk losing our national identity and world standing as the proverbial "Land of the Free and Home of the Brave."[13] Our young people cannot be "free" if they are permanently harmed for making mistakes while maturing; and we cannot collectively be not "brave" if we fail to rehabilitate those who need us most: our children. Ultimately, as Madiba, also known as Mandela, suggests in his quote above, the way we deal with the problems highlighted here will ultimately reveal to ourselves who we are as a nation.

In carrying out the research that I lay out below, I resist Harvard University Distinguished Social Sciences Professor Robert Sampson's fresh challenge to researchers to evaluate incarceration's "social ledger" —in keeping with which the benefits and detriments linked to confinement should face a balanced analysis.[14]

---

[13] To learn more about America's failure to live up to its proclamation as "the land of the free and home of the brave," see Beal, Frances M. "Black women's manifesto; double jeopardy: To be black and female." *New York: Third World Women's Alliance* (1969).

[14] Sampson writes that new research regarding the effects of incarceration "should turn to the more rigorous study of the heterogeneous effects of incarceration that take into account the multiple and complex pathways through which incarceration transmits its influences." By "heterogeneous effects," Sampson is referring to "incarceration's costs and benefits." Sampson, Robert J. "The

I take issue with evaluating the merits, and in turn glorifying, any practice that harms our most valuable resource: young people.

C. Research Questions

The research questions guiding my analysis encompass: (1) what are the post-incarceration needs of youth with sociophysiological challenges and those who are African-American; (2) what barriers do these youth face in their efforts to reintegrate in American society; (3) how can these barriers be *broadly* overcome; (4) what *specific* legal reforms would facilitate the surmounting of obstacles?

D. Research Design

i. Breaking with Conventional and Myopic Legal Scholarship

Legal scholarship has traditionally followed two conventions. The first, stressing 'black-letter law', presumes that the law itself constitutes a self-supporting body of principles that researchers can learn and master without taking stock of any context-related issues, by reading judicial opinions and statutes along with other legislative tools with no regard for the world existing outside of law.

Labelled "doctrinal analysis," and conducted in courtrooms, law school classrooms, law review articles, casebooks, and treatises, this

---

incarceration ledger." *Criminology & Public Policy* 10, no. 3 (2011): 819-828. Fundamentally, I take issue with this call, given that any positive effects associated with incarceration could be realized in other ways, which can be less prone to inflicting long-term damage on people who have all supposedly violated our society's laws.

form of analysis "involves the careful reading and comparison of appellate opinions with a view to identifying ambiguities, exposing inconsistencies, among cases and lines of cases, developing distinctions, reconciling holdings, and otherwise exercising the characteristic skills of legal analysis."[15] Researchers writing in this tradition deduct principles from judicial opinions and statutes to organize them into a framework that reflects theoretical consistency and make prescriptions. Not only has this type of scholarship been in decline for decades,[16] it suffers from a critical flaw by denying a basic fact: that "Legal institutions cannot be understood without seeing the entire social environment."[17]

Another tradition, which began in the 1960s, posits that the starting point for knowledge-building scholarship that is worthwhile is not law; instead, it lies with societal problems influenced by the law.[18] In keeping with this tradition, the law itself can serve as a source of problems because it may contribute to, cause, or fail to solve, societal issues of the two traditions, I take issue with the former (i.e., doctrinal analysis), being more

[15] Posner, Richard A. "The present situation in legal scholarship." *The Yale Law Journal* 90, no. 5 (1981): 1113-1130.

[16] Posner, Richard A. "The decline of law as an autonomous discipline: 1962-1987." *Harv. L. Rev.* 100 (1986): 761.

[17] Silbey, Susan S., and Austin Sarat. "Critical traditions in law and society research." *Law and Society Review* (1987): 165-174.

[18] *See, e.g.,* Tomlins, Christopher. "How autonomous is law?." *Annu. Rev. Law Soc. Sci.* 3 (2007): 45-68.

arbitrary,[19] and no more rigorous,[20] than the latter —recognizing that doctrinal research is too limited in its scope and applicability to societal problems that largely transcend the law. Pure doctrinal analysis amounts to little more than an unbending and myopic approach towards grasping the realities of any country's legal system. Given the limits of the first tradition, I will use a methodology that falls in line with the second convention, by focusing on the problems that laws have failed to solve concerning youth with sociophysiological challenges and of African-American origin.

ii. Making the Case for a Qualitative Approach

Finding answers to the four research questions laid out above, relating to youth's post-incarceration needs, barriers and their solutions, and legal reforms, calls for a carefully designed research project with lessons, which lawmakers and others can use to shape incarceration and reintegration policies affecting delinquent youth. Conscious of the discipline-appropriate approaches that scholars have relied on to carry

[19] Unger, Roberto Mangabeira. *What should legal analysis become?*. Verso, 1996: 111.

[20] Legal doctrine, being the currency of the law, can take different forms —"it may be fact-dependent, and therefore limited, or sweeping in its breath." Tiller, Emerson H., and Frank B. Cross. "What is legal doctrine." *Nw. UL Rev.* 100 (2006): 517. Many of the generalizations that it hinges are not backed up by empirical findings or stem from a method of inquiry that approximates the rigors of the scientific method. This is true despite eminent scholars' claim that jurisprudence is "the science of law." *See, e.g.*, Loevinger, Lee. "Jurimetrics: The methodology of legal inquiry." *Law and contemporary problems* 28, no. 1 (1963): 5-35.

out criminological research,[21] I aim to make useful, though limited, knowledge-building contributions —using a qualitative research method that relies on data.

This method seems more fitting than a quantitative approach[22] because the data surrounding the different issues explored in this work are scarce and varied enough that they would not stand up to the rigors of the experimental component of most quantitative designs.[23]

---

[21] *See, e.g.*, Noaks, Lesley, and Emma Wincup. *Criminological research: Understanding qualitative methods.* Sage, 2004 (offering chapters on the construct, politics, and ethical aspects, of the qualitative methods to criminological research relying on qualitative data, case studies, and interviews that adhere to the protocols of ethnographic analysis).

[22] Informed by the writings of a number of academics, I conclude that a qualitative research method and its quantitative counterpart can be complementary elements in criminology-oriented legal research, as opposed to competitors. Most importantly, I also understand that, with regard to choosing a methodological approach, the chief consideration ought to revolve around the method's appropriateness vis-à- vis the problem(s) under investigation —rather than picking sides between the quantitative and qualitative camps. In determining appropriateness, I considered, among others, the knowledge base, level of analysis, socio-cultural context, and resources at my disposal: financially, in terms of available data, and otherwise. *See, e.g.*, Berring, Robert C. "Legal research and legal concepts: Where form molds substance." *Cal. L. Rev.* 75 (1987): 15. Cohen, Morris, and Kent Olson. *Legal research in a nutshell.* West Academic, 2016. Noaks, Lesley, and Emma Wincup. *Criminological research: Understanding qualitative methods.* Sage, 2004. Jupp, Victor R., and Victor Jupp. *Methods of criminological research.* Routledge, 2012.

[23] *See, e.g.*, Neuman, William Lawrence, and Bruce Wiegand. *Criminal justice research methods: Qualitative and quantitative approaches.* Boston: Allyn and Bacon, 2000 (advancing seven chapters that that address the use of quantitative data and the appropriateness of quantitative research designs).

E. Scholarly Significance

Though some legal scholars and criminal justice reform advocates have written extensively about the issues plaguing the facility-to-community transition encounters of formerly incarcerated youth, no author has contributed a double-barreled assessment, highlighting the community reentry experiences and needs of (1) youth with sociophysiological challenges and (2) African-American juveniles. In reaching this conclusion, I combed through numerous works and databases —finding that: while some scholars have studied the transition-based barriers facing formerly incarcerated young people, only a small number has exclusively focused on the experiences of particular subgroups.

Of the ones who have concentrated on subgroups, they did so in the pursuit of research questions that differ(ed) from the ones I outlined above.

F. Detailing a Roadmap for What Is to Come

Having introduced the subject under consideration, I have thus far discussed the methodology to be relied upon —comprising, among others, thesis and problem statements, research questions, research design, and scholarly significance. Next, I will provide a restricted review of the literature, analyzing a number of term definitions, conceptual gaps, and general observations regarding youth criminality.

Thereafter, I will consider background information, relying on two case studies to illustrate the experiences of the two groups of youth whose experiences are at issue, and detail some barriers to reintegration. Some of these obstacles will deal with issues in the educational arena, for youth with sociophysiological challenges, while others will address intergenerational incarceration and identity matters. Finally, before bringing the work to its conclusion, I will lay out some solutions and legal reforms to tackle the stumbling blocks facing youth with sociophysiological challenges and of African-American origin.

CHAPTER III

LITERATURE REVIEW

This section consists of two definitional sections, focusing on defining: (1) sociophysiological challenges, by looking at how academics perceive disability, or dis/ability, and (2) blackness, by weighing whether the African-American and black labels are accurate. I will conclude by visiting general observations regarding youth criminality and dissecting conceptual gaps in the literature.

A. Definitions

i. Defining Sociophysiological Challenges: How Do Scholars Perceive Dis/ability?

Any research project concerned with the experiences of youth with sociophysiological challenges should start with a review of the way in which academics and members of the general public have thought about and discussed the concept of dis/ability. In this regard, dis/ability has figured as a phenomenon that is above all medical. Relying on this perception, medical professionals, such as psychiatrists, have treated individuals with sociophysiological challenges as people who suffer from a medical issue.[24] Researchers have termed this perception "the medical model of disability."[25] This model "has long been the dominant paradigm for understanding disability."[26]

Contra the notion that dis/ability is on the whole medical, some scholars have argued that it instead is a social construction.[27] In so doing, these academics formulated an idea known as "the disablement/impairment binary."[28] In line with this binary, "disablement" represents the aspects of dis/ability that result from social construction. Impairment, however, describes the bodies that various conditions with sociophysiological implications have affected.[29] Through separating physiological impairment and social disablement, the dis/ability binary strengthens the notion that dis/ability has a biological root. This idea in turn undercuts dis/ability rights by reinforcing the

[24] Areheart, Bradley A. "Disability Trouble." Yale Law & Policy Review, 29, (2011): 347 (citing Johnson, *Mary. Make them go away: Clint Eastwood, Christopher Reeve and the case against disability rights*. Advocado Press, 2003: 27).

[25] Areheart, Bradley A. "When disability isn't just right: the entrenchment of the medical model of disability and the goldilocks dilemma." *Ind. LJ* 83 (2008): 181.

[26] *Ibid.*

[27] Declaring an entity to be a "social construction," constitutes emphasizing its reliance on the varying aspects of our social selves, as human beings. The diametrical opposite of "social constructions" comprise objects that naturally exist, independent of humanity and free from the interactional influences of its members.

[28] *Ibid.*

[29] Oliver, Michael. "The Politics of Disablement: A Sociological Approach (Critical Texts in Social Work and the Welfare State)." (1990): 11.

narrow and primitive ways of perceiving dis/ability.

Broadly speaking, other researchers authoring works on dis/ability have focused on (1) two broad categories of sociophysiological challenges and (2) the consequences of disabling conditions for youth.

These two classifications encompass: visible and non-visible dis/abilities. Observable dis/abilities, being visually detectable, must therefore be classed as visible. In contrast, dis/abilities that are less obvious and thus require more time to spot are non-visible. Results from at least 11 studies[30] have indicated that visibility matters when it comes to dis/abilities, along with gender. Both of these factors matter when it comes to how disabling conditions impact the lives of those coping with disabling conditions. For instance, scholars have found that youth with sociophysiological challenges, those that are visible and non-visible, face bullying more than their peers without dis/abilities and that young men experience bullying more often than young women.[31] Reported types of bullying constitute

[30] *See, e.g.*, DePauw, Karen P. "The (1n) visibility of disability: cultural contexts and "Sporting Bodies"." *Quest* 49, no. 4 (1997): 416-430; Blum, Linda M. "Mother-blame in the Prozac nation: Raising kids with invisible disabilities." *Gender & Society* 21, no. 2 (2007): 202-226; Dale Stone, Sharon. "Reactions to invisible disability: the experiences of young women survivors of hemorrhagic stroke." *Disability and rehabilitation* 27, no. 6 (2005): 293-304.

[31] *See, e.g.*, Swearer, Susan M., Dorothy L. Espelage, Tracy Vaillancourt, and Shelley Hymel. "What can be done about school bullying? Linking research to educational practice." *Educational researcher* 39, no. 1 (2010): 38-47; Zeedyk, S. M., G. Rodriguez, L. A. Tipton, B. L. Baker, and J. Blacher. "Bullying of youth with autism spectrum disorder, intellectual disability, or typical development: victim and

teasing, name-calling, and physical assaults of youth with sociophysiological challenges.[32]

In terms of the consequences of disabling conditions for youth, within the literature, it is well-known that young people facing physiological challenges figure disproportionately in delinquency facilities[33]. Scholars in this field of research appear to largely espouse the consensus that educators, prison officials, and other groups, fail to provide students with dis/abilities with the special education, and related, services that federal law guarantees them —in and outside of juvenile delinquency facilities.[34]

ii. Defining Blackness: Are African-American and Black, As Labels, Accurate?

Despite their imbedding in academic writing and general discourse, umbrella terms such

parent perspectives." *Research in autism spectrum disorders* 8, no. 9 (2014): 1173-1183.

[32] Carter, Bonnie B., and Vicky G. Spencer. "The fear factor: Bullying and students with disabilities." *International Journal of Special Education* 21, no. 1 (2006): 11-23.

[33] See Wibbelink, Carlijn JM, Machteld Hoeve, Geert Jan JM Stams, and Frans J. Oort. "A meta-analysis of the association between mental disorders and juvenile recidivism." *Aggression and violent behavior* 33 (2017): 78-90.

[34] Lipscomb, Stephen, Joshua Haimson, Albert Y. Liu, John Burghardt, David R. Johnson, and Martha Thurlow. *Preparing for Life After High School: The Characteristics and Experiences of Youth in Special Education. Findings from the National Longitudinal Transition Study 2012. Volume 1: Comparisons with Other Youth (Full Report).* No. a16b0d64d0d04173b3289e0ff54b53ef. Mathematica Policy Research, 2017.

as "African-American" or "black," which I use here interchangeably, are at least imperfect — if not devaluing and just flat out inaccurate — in light of the existence of significant diversity within the African-American community.[35] This societal subgroup comprises a number of different African-descent populations in the U.S. In light of this reality, a vigorous scholarly debate concerning the use of African-American and black terms for African-descent populations should emerge in the mainstream.[36]

B. General Observations Regarding Youth Criminality

In criminology books and journals, researchers have presented an array of reasons to explain youth's offenses: age;[37] a type of irrationality labelled "akrasia," standing for an absence, or lack of, self-control or weakness of the will;[38] and calculated

---

[35] *See, e.g.*, Sellers, Robert M., Mia A. Smith, J. Nicole Shelton, Stephanie AJ Rowley, and Tabbye M. Chavous. "Multidimensional model of racial identity: A reconceptualization of African American racial identity." *Personality and Social Psychology Review* 2, no. 1 (1998): 18-39; Brunsma, David L. "Interracial families and the racial identification of mixed-race children: Evidence from the early childhood longitudinal study." *Social Forces* 84, no. 2 (2005): 1131-1157.

[36] Agyemang, Charles, Raj Bhopal, and Marc Bruijnzeels. "Negro, Black, Black African, African Caribbean, African American or what? Labelling African origin populations in the health arena in the 21st century." *Journal of epidemiology and community health* 59, no. 12 (2005): 1014-1018.

[37] Warr, Mark. "Age, peers, and delinquency." *Criminology* 31, no. 1 (1993): 17-40.

[38] Brezina, Timothy. "Assessing the rationality of criminal and delinquent behavior: a focus on actual utility." *Rational choice and criminal behavior: Recent research and future challenges* (2002): 244-264.

choices aimed at maximizing utility, as manifested in monetary and hedonistic terms.[39] Aside from these causal factors, other scholars have cited, as causes for youth criminality: obstacles encountered in the conventional pursuit of personal goals[40] and peer pressure.[41] Another school of thought proposes that while minor offending acts are pervasive and typical, lawmakers criminalize them to make social control legitimate.[42]

A large number of the criminological models and conjectures, such as strain theory, have since the 1950's accentuated people's thwarted aspirations towards traditional values and goals. The thwarting, in some instances, is linked to personal characteristics borne out of deficits that are biological and social in nature. Such deficits encompass inadequate self-control or an inability to socialize.

In addition, these inadequacies may emerge because of: (1) ill-advised moral reasoning, as contended by espousers of theories that highlight social control or rational choice; (2) low status or positionality in the social hierarchy, as subcultural theorists contend; or (3) an absence of social bonds, marked by a deprivation of status and achievement.

---

[39] Cernkovich, Stephen A. "Evaluating Two Models of Delinquency Causation-Structural Theory and Control Theory." *Criminology* 16 (1978): 335.

[40] Quicker, John C. "The effect of goal discrepancy on delinquency." *Social Problems* 22, no. 1 (1974): 76-86.

[41] Sullivan, Christopher J. "Early adolescent delinquency: Assessing the role of childhood problems, family environment, and peer pressure." *Youth Violence and Juvenile Justice* 4, no. 4 (2006): 291-313.

[42] Cohen, Stanley. Visions of social control: *Crime, punishment and classification*. Cambridge: Polity Press, 1985: chapter 3.

In the recent past, academics who subscribe to the tenets of cultural criminology and labelling theory have held that the markers assigned to individuals, such as "criminal," might contribute to increases in marginalization and the number of crimes that youth commit.[43] Some theorists have suggested, convincingly, that poverty and inequality have limited youth's access to opportunities.[44] For young people, inadequate practices in the realm of parenting, poor socialization skills, peer pressure, and economic ups and downs in the form of income shocks have led to a "drifting" between conventional mores and delinquency.[45]

C. On Analyzing Conceptual Gaps in the Literature

Unfortunately, the literature regarding the inception of offending behavior has a number of limitations. First, the literature has not accommodated the temporal, cultural and social determinants that influence offending behavior. Another flaw found in the literature pertains to the fact that few theories of crime to date apply to women's offending or the fact that youth delinquency control is mainly a male-oriented enterprise. Researchers and policymakers have largely ignored female offending in light of its low infrequency.

---

[43] *See, e.g.*, Bernburg, Jon Gunnar, Marvin D. Krohn, and Craig J. Rivera. "Official labeling, criminal embeddedness, and subsequent delinquency: A longitudinal test of labeling theory." *Journal of Research in Crime and Delinquency* 43, no. 1 (2006): 67-88.

[44] Kennedy, Bruce P., Ichiro Kawachi, Deborah Prothrow-Stith, Kimberly Lochner, and Vanita Gupta. "Social capital, income inequality, and firearm violent crime." *Social science & medicine* 47, no. 1 (1998): 7-17.

[45] Matza, David. *Drift*. J. Wiley, 1964.

Two more flaws abound. Third, perspectives that focus on youth development have downplayed, or outright neglected, the socio-political implications of age and youth transitions. While age can be crucial in understanding offending behaviors, there exist external, and primarily power-related, implications of youth transitions that have been unexplored or dismissed in criminological research.[46] Finally, a large number of research projects in the field of criminology is substantively agenda-driven.

To do away with these corrigible flaws, researchers should broaden their analytical perspectives to incorporate the experiences of all formerly incarcerated youth in transition from juvenile delinquency facilities to their respective communities.

---

[46] *See, e.g.*, Matsueda, Ross L., and Karen Heimer. "A symbolic interactionist theory of role-transitions, role-commitments, and delinquency." *Developmental theories of crime and delinquency* (1997): 163-213.

CHAPTER IV

BACKGROUND

Having covered the relevant literature and exposed four of its biggest flaws, this "background" section will intentionally connect this work's introduction, which alludes to Mandela's prison experiences, to incarceration-related issues in the U.S. —especially as they pertain to the juvenile incarceration debate. Then, I will analyze underlying factors of youth incarceration and the incarceration experiences of youth with sociophysiological challenges. Thereafter, I will examine black youth and their incarceration journeys —using two case studies. Finally, I will make sense of my presentation of the case studies by detailing their significance for this research project.

A. Building Conceptual Connections: Mandela, U.S. Mass Incarceration, and the Juvenile Incarceration Debate

Connecting the damage that prison conceivably inflicted on Mandela, to the experience of present-day Americans are two somber facts. One: despite its known and mounting psychological costs, the isolation, or solitary confinement, that Mandela endured in apartheid South Africa remains an everyday punishment across numerous American prisons.[47] Presumably, this raises eyebrows in ethics-oriented circles,[48] as solitary confinement carries dire short- *and long-term* psychological consequences for prisoners.[49] Second: America is presently confining African-American men, young and old, at a proportion

[47] "On an average day in 2011–12, up to 4.4% of state and federal inmates and 2.7% of jail inmates were held in administrative segregation or solitary confinement. Nearly 20% of prison inmates and 18% of jail inmates had spent time in restrictive housing, including disciplinary or administrative segregation or solitary confinement, in the past 12 months or since coming to their current facility, if shorter." Beck, Allen J. "Use of restrictive housing in US prisons and jails, 2011-12." *US Department of Justice, Bureau of Justice Statistics* (2015). These numbers, although being low in part, should get as close to zero as possible, given what psychiatrists and others have discovered about solitary confinement. If our society's objective is to rehabilitate prisoners, prison officials should not seek to impair these people, especially if doing so has negative long-term effects. *Ibid.*

[48] *See, e.g.*, Metzner, Jeffrey L., and Jamie Fellner. "Solitary confinement and mental illness in US prisons: A challenge for medical ethics." (2010).

[49] *See, e.g.*, Arrigo, Bruce A., and Jennifer Leslie Bullock. "The psychological effects of solitary confinement on prisoners in supermax units reviewing what we know and recommending what should change." *International Journal of Offender Therapy and Comparative Criminology* 52, no. 6 (2008): 622-640 (examining the psychological effects of solitary confinement for U.S. inmates, in the short- and long-term, coping with administrative and disciplinary segregation —devoting attention to incarceration officials' use of secure housing units, also called control or supermax units); Grassian, Stuart. "Psychopathological effects of solitary confinement." *American Journal of Psychiatry* 140, no. 11 (1983): 1450-1454 (detailing a host of psychiatric symptoms that 14 inmates experienced after exposure to increased time periods in solitary confinement and finding that these symptoms amount to "a major, clinically distinguishable psychiatric syndrome").

roughly four times the rate of incarceration of black men during apartheid in South Africa.[50] Instead of enacting measures that place these men on a leveled playing field with their largely more privileged Caucasian, or white, counterparts —whose ancestors faced neither slavery nor Jim crow —the country is punishing African-Americans unequally for their mistakes.

Although this section does not focus on solitary confinement, put broadly, it portrays the incarceration of two over-represented groups of formerly-incarcerated juveniles: youth with sociophysiological and of African-American origin. Just as blacks were over-represented among jail and prison populations during apartheid South Africa,[51] members of these two groups are today over-represented among the formerly-confined young people reentering society.[52] This parallel shows the merit of alluding to Mandela's prison experiences.

[50] Haney, Craig, and Philip Zimbardo. "The past and future of US prison policy: Twenty-five years after the Stanford Prison Experiment." *American Psychologist* 53, no. 7 (1998): 709.

[51] Although statistics regarding the number of inmates in South African prisons during apartheid are hard to track, William H. Worger, a University of California-Los Angeles professor of history specializing in South Africa's social and economic history, reports that "The incarceration rate in South Africa in 1984 – the midst of apartheid – was 440 persons imprisoned per 100,000 population. Blacks comprised around 94 percent of those incarcerated." Greenberg, Jon. "Kristof: U.S. imprisons blacks at rates higher than South Africa during apartheid." PunditFact of Politifact.com, Tampa Bay Times. December 11, 2014. Accessed May 12, 2017. http://www.politifact.com/punditfact/statements/2014/dec/11/nicholas-kristof/kristof-us-imprisons-blacks-rates-higher-south-afr/

[52] Quinn et al., *supra*, note 11; The Sentencing Project, *supra*, note 12.

B. On Analyzing an Underlying Factor of Youth Incarceration

For research concerning any phenomenon to progress systematically, its originator(s) must start with root factors that facilitate linear thinking and help readers to determine if a multi-level understanding of the research issue(s) exists. To satisfy this requirement vis-à-vis this work's principal issue, i.e., the reentry of youth who were formerly incarcerated, I address, in this section, one of the chief contributing factors of youth incarceration — intergenerational, or parental, incarceration. The second-hand costs of incarceration can undoubtedly be far-reaching. The most obvious worry is that incarceration's ripple effects may hurt those who are locked up, their communities, and families, including children of locked up parents.

I discuss intergenerational incarceration here by only scratching the surface, as youth with sociophysiological challenges are barely affected by it, in contrast to their counterparts: youth of African-American origin. Given that intergenerational incarceration remarkably affects African-American youth, as black men are highly overrepresented among the U.S. adult population of prisoners, later on I elaborate in greater detail on its consequences for African-American youth —and even went as far as to label it one of the barriers thwarting the community re-entry of African-American youth who were formerly incarcerated.

The general discussion of intergenerational incarceration here is beneficial because it explains the roots of youth incarceration, unmasking the perils that predate incarceration for both groups: youth with sociophysiological challenges and of African-American origin. It also sheds light on the general harms present in the environment(s) within which some formerly incarcerated juveniles seek to make their reentry. Finally, in order for this research project to succeed in suitably prescribing solutions and reforms, a good grasp of the causes of, or correlational factors leading to, youth incarceration is indispensable.

Given that many offender juveniles have parents who were incarcerated or formerly incarcerated,[53] they grapple with the weight of not only the intersecting of socioeconomic factors but also the intergenerational effects of mass incarceration once transitioning from penal facilities to their communities. Before these young people committed crimes and served time in jails or prisons, according to some scholars,[54] they were exposed to parental incarceration and behavioral outcomes —requiring the analysis that makes up section that immediately follows. It is important to highlight that the focus here are the experiences of the young people and not the parents.

Since this work is concerned with improving the reentry experiences of formerly incarcerated youth, some readers may wonder: why bother with a discussion about incarcerated parents and

---

[53] Reed, Diane F., and Edward L. Reed. "Children of incarcerated parents." Social Justice 24, no. 3 (69 (1997): 152-169.

[54] *See, e.g.*, Johnson, Rucker C. "Intergenerational risks of criminal involvement and incarceration." *Unpublished manuscript, Goldman School of Public Policy, University of California, Berkeley* (2007) (finding, among others, that: (1) the disparities between black, white, and other races of, Americans in lifetime incarceration risks are disquieting; (2) family and/or neighborhood backgrounds greatly affect youth criminal involvement and risks of facing detention; and (3) "that 20 percent of black children had a father with an incarceration history; and among black children with fathers who did not graduate from high school, an alarming 33 percent of their father's had an incarceration history").

their children? According to Richard Trembley, a Stockholm Criminology Prize[55] winner, in order to fully understand what successful community reentry looks like, it is crucial to think carefully about the re-entry process from the bottom up.[56] Tremblay argues implicitly that the outcomes of reentry stem in part from juveniles' developmental experiences. By the time youth are in their teenage years, interventions become more expensive and less effective than they would have been had policymakers and rehabilitation officials tackled the phenomenon early on.

C. Examining Youth with Sociophysiological Challenges and their Incarceration Experiences

Educated estimates run the gamut when it comes to the size of the youth population with sociophysiological challenges who are locked up in the juvenile penal system. For instance, special education researchers

[55] The Stockholm Prize in Criminology is a well-known and highly-respected award, issued by a multi-person international jury, that highlights the work of researchers ushering in substantial developments in criminological research. The world's leading scholar in linking, through rigorous research processes, biological and social factors in human development and their contribution to crime, namely Richard E. Tremblay, received this year's (2017) prize. Stockholm University. "The Stockholm Prize in Criminology." På svenska. Accessed May 14, 2017. http://www.su.se/english/about/prizes-awards/the-stockholm-prize-in-criminology/price-recipient-2017-1.309600; Carrey, Normand. "Interview with Dr. Richard Tremblay, PhD." *Journal of the Canadian Academy of Child and Adolescent Psychiatry*, National Center for Biotechnology Information, 2010. Accessed May 12, 2017. https://www.ncbi.nlm.nih.gov/pmc/articles/PMC3085675/

[56] Stockholm University. The Stockholm Prize in Criminology Announcement Tape Recording. *Symposium Website*. Stockholm, Sweden, 2017. Accessed May 12, 2017. http://www.su.se/english/about/prizes-awards/the-stockholm-prize-in-criminology

Lyndal Bullock and Patrick McArthur claim that the special education dis/abilities prevalence between members of this population is 4 to 5 times higher than the special education dis/abilities rate in the general population.[57] This estimate is somewhat in keeping with statistical surveys that approximate between 20% and more than 60% of youth in juvenile penal facilities have a dis/ability.[58]

Undergirding the inconsistencies in dis/ability prevalence estimations are reasons that encompass: (1) varying disability definitions; (2) deficient special education testing processes in public schools and youth penal facilities; and (3) obstacles in putting into operation special education programs in penal settings because of lack of funding and staffing for special education initiatives.[59] Disability definitions and eligibility criteria differ among states. Federal law establishes minimum eligibility standards and states may enact different, and more embracing, criteria for who suffer from dis/abilities.[60]

---

[57] Bullock, Lyndal M., and Patrick McArthur. "Correctional special education: Disability prevalence estimates and teacher preparation programs." *Education and Treatment of Children* (1994): 347-355.

[58] Quinn et al., *supra* note 11.

[59] Nelson, C. Michael, Robert B. Rutherford Jr, David B. Center, and Hill M. Walker. "Do public schools have an obligation to serve troubled children and youth?." *Exceptional Children* 57, no. 5 (1991): 406-415.

[60] Rutherford, R. B., Michael Bullis, Cindy W. Anderson, and Heather M. Griller-Clark. "Youth with disabilities in the correctional system: Prevalence rates and identification issues." *Washington, DC: Office of Juvenile Justice and Delinquency Prevention* (2002).

i. Case Study 1: The Blade Reese Case

Wabash, Indiana — Behind every crime headline lurks a heap of tragedy for everyone involved, particularly children. Wabash Valley Correctional Facility, a 530-acre chain-linked-fenced complex, houses more than 2,000 men, some of them headline makers, incarcerated for crimes of different calibers —from arson to homicide.[61] Unlike some other adult correctional facilities across America, Wabash comprises a cell block that houses dozens of children sentenced as adults:[62] ill-equipped for the experiential obstacles lying before them. One of the inmates locked up at Wabash is Blade Reed: a young man convicted of committing "Robbery with Severe Bodily Injury,"[63] a Level 2 felony punishable by 10 to 30 years in Indiana's prisons.

At Wabash, the walk from across the prison yard to the chow hall is nothing more than what prisoners have to do to get breakfast. Every morning, once a set of heavy iron doors slide open, inmates at Wabash rush into the twilight looking to fill their empty stomachs. For Blade Reed, housed in the cell block for juvenile convicts, walking to the chow hall imaginably holds subliminal meaning. It allows Blade to bask in the invigorating morning air uninhibited

[61] Indiana Department of Corrections. "WABASH VALLEY CORRECTIONAL FACILITY HISTORY.": Wabash Valley Correctional Facility History. Accessed February 12, 2017. http://www.in.gov/idoc/3226.htm.

[62] *Ibid.*

[63] Lane, Laura. "Blade Reed, 14, sentenced to 30 years in home invasion, attack." *Herald Times Online*, December 7, 2009. Accessed February 12, 2017. http://ww.heraldtimesonline.com/stories/2009/12/07/news.qp-3072806.sto

—away from the suffocating boundaries of a cell that is the size of a walk-in closet and breathing fresh air, un-swapped among hundreds of confined bodies.

Before Blade makes his way to breakfast each morning, he careens past a row of dimly-lit 5-by-7 foot cells: guarded by paint-chipped steel bars so large they resemble iron cudgels. The hallway leading to Wabash's yard from below Blade's cell spans 40 yards in length and 5 in width: a cramped space for dozens of young men to hustle and bustle about.[64] When breakfast ends, through a sea of chatter, Blade makes his way through the unnerving chaos: bidding his friends good-bye by exchanging fist bumps. He makes little to no eye contact and struggles with words, being "developmentally and cognitively disabled."[65] While walking back to his cell, Blade glances over his shoulder and searches for flying fists or sudden hushes of noise that would silence the cacophony. The miasma of unwashed bodies, of young men bedraggled, pervades the air. With the coast clear the entire way back, Blade reenters his stucco-plastered cell.

The last time Reed was outside of Wabash was years ago, when he was a middle-schooler. On a fateful day, he and another boy had taken

---

[64] Merenova, Elena V. "A Comparison of Early Childhood Recollections of Repetitive Self-mutilators and Non-self-mutilators in a State Prison Population." *PhD Diss., Indiana State University* (2001).

[65] The Redemption Project. "End the torture of autistic juvenile Blade Reed in the Wabash Prison." Change.Org Petition, Petitioning Indiana Dept. of Corrections Commissioner Bruce Lemon and 7 others. (Indiana, 2012). Accessed March 4, 2017. https://www.change.org/p/end-the-torture-of-autistic-juvenile-blade-reed-in-the-wabash-prison.

off on their bicycles intending to steal beer from an elderly couple, both of whom were his neighbors.[66] Physically and sexually abused as a child, and raised in foster care, Blade shocked Helmsburg: a town in Central Indiana where he had spent part of his short life. He severed a woman's neck with a kitchen knife, not wanting to leave behind a talking witness. Wielding a stolen .25 caliber handgun, his older brother Bennie, 17, shot a bullet that killed Dude Voland, an armed-forces veteran and former pipefitter, and another striking Dude's wife, Mary, in her stomach. With Mary surviving, Blade received for his part a 30-year sentence, of which he will serve only half: 15 years. His brother, on the other hand, received a sentence of 60 years of imprisonment for murder and aggravated assault.

D. Analyzing Black Youth and their Incarceration Journeys

As confirmed by a number of studies, racial disparities plague the way in which America treats its young men and women. Fifteen years ago, the National Research Council and Institute of Medicine published a book finding that major disparities existed in the involvement of minority youth in the juvenile delinquency system, particularly African-Americans, in contrast with white youth.[67] In line with this conclusion, other scholars[68] have documented

[66] Lane, *supra* note 61.

[67] National Research Council. *Juvenile crime, juvenile justice*. National Academies Press, 2001: 228.

[68] *See, e.g.*, Engen, Rodney L., Sara Steen, and George S. Bridges. "Racial disparities in the punishment of youth: A theoretical and empirical assessment of the literature." *Social Problems* 49, no. 2 (2002): 194-220; Bishop, Donna M., and Michael J. Leiber. "Racial

this unbalanced representation of African-Americans in jails and prisons.

This overrepresentation raises questions of fairness about the functioning of the juvenile delinquency system and concerning the life-course trajectories of many young people in minority communities. As recently as four years ago, "black juveniles were more than four times as likely to be committed as white juveniles" whereas "American Indian [or Native American] juveniles were more than three times as likely and Hispanic [or Latin/x] juveniles...61 percent more likely"[69] than their white counterparts to find themselves caught in America's penal trap for juveniles.[70] Such discriminatory treatment of incarcerated persons, whether intentional or accidental, is not without historical precedent.

For nearly four decades, from the mid-1970s to 2010, the prison population of the United States mushroomed, marking a growth that was historically-unprecedented.[71] Of those disproportionately affected by mass incarceration are black Americans. Michelle Alexander, a renowned legal scholar in this area and black civil rights lawyer, writes that, "Today there are more African-Americans under correctional control, in prison or jail, on probation or parole, than were enslaved in 1850, a decade before the Civil War began."[72] The level of discrimination experienced

---

and ethnic differences in delinquency and justice system responses." (2012).

[69] Rovner, J. "Racial Disparities in Youth Commitments and Arrests" (2016).

[70] *Ibid.*

[71] Pfaff, John F. "The complicated economics of prison reform." *Mich. L. Rev.* 114 (2015): 951.

[72] Giroux, Henry A. *Youth in revolt: Reclaiming a democratic fu-*

by black Americans has proven to be so severe that Alexander also remarks that, “In major American cities today, more than half of working-age African-American men are either under correctional control or branded felons and are thus subject to legalized discrimination for the rest of their lives.”[73] For instance, in Chicago: one of the most ghettoized cities in America, while black men, aged 15 to 64, are 27.3% of the residential population, they represent 70.3% of all inmates in jails.[74]

i. Case Study 2: The Harry Saintil Case

Blade’s peno-judicial foray, or journey across different court and incarceration systems, contrasts and compares with that of Harry, a former best friend of mine who jumped to his death after having served a stint at a correctional facility in Massachusetts. A few days after his eighteenth birthday, he and another boy got arrested for allegedly selling narcotics near a schoolyard.

This was Harry’s first offense and he had not physically nor directly harmed anyone. He had

ture. Routledge, 2015:63 (citing “Michelle Alexander: ‘A System of Racial and Social Control’.” Interview by Sarah Childress. Frontline. April 29, 2014. Accessed May 12, 2017. http://www.pbs.org/wgbh/frontline/article/michelle-alexander-a-system-of-racial-and-social-control/)

[73] Michelle Alexander: ‘A System of Racial and Social Control’.” Interview by Sarah Childress. Frontline. April 29, 2014. Accessed May 12, 2017. http://www.pbs.org/wgbh/frontline/article/michelle-alexander-a-system-of-racial-and-social-control/

[74] Vera Institute of Justice. Incarceration Trends: Cook County, IL Jail incarceration. Accessed May 12, 2017. http://trends.vera.org/rates/cook-county-il?incarceration=disparity&incarcerationSource=black.

gone to the schoolyard against his will, thinking that he was helping a former schoolmate get a "loan" from a friend, who turned out to be an undercover cop. Despite these mitigating factors, the judge sentenced Harry to more than 5 years behind bars. The accomplice to whom the drugs belonged received no jail time because, among other things, a witness could not positively identify him. Given that Harry kept to himself and spoke little English, among the folks in Mattapan, Massachusetts, particularly Haitian-Americans, his case had quickly become an emblem of what many see as a draconian, no-questions-asked, criminal justice system.

A few years before he passed away, it looked as if Harry was piecing his life back together. He had earned a General Education Diploma (G.E.D.), took some classes at a local community college, and tried finding a job. Despite his best efforts to shake off the scarlet letter that was his criminal record, Harry continued to struggle. One evening, Harry leaped into the Charles River, an 80-mile long body of water connecting tens of Massachusettsian towns to the Atlantic Ocean.

Not knowing how to swim, Harry drowned a short while later. Having spent countless of hours with Harry and his family members, it seemed like he could not recover from the psychological trauma stemming from spending years locked alone in a cell for all but one hour a day. Once out of prison, Harry virtually refashioned the conditions of solitary —locking himself alone in his bedroom for extended periods of time. Also, he grew uneasy hanging around people, particularly in large groups.

For the last year of his life, Harry had lived in the same place: in a room in a three-story house, or "Triple-Decker" located in an immigrant community predominated by public housing, single-family homes, and small apartment buildings. He was the oldest of five siblings. When Harry was ten, his father, who made a living as a cook, had moved out, even though he kept supporting him through giving him a weekly allowance. Struggling to pay rent and put food on the table, Harry started sleeping in abandoned buildings until he got a job as an apprentice at an auto-mechanic shop that allowed him to better support himself. For high school, Harry went to the large, under-resourced Hyde Park High School.

In prison, Harry had understood that he would not be making lots of friends. He was placed to a cell block housing violent criminals, ranging from arsonists to murderers. While incarcerated, Harry's life changed. One minute, he was at recreation playing cards with inmates. The next minute, he had received mail informing him that his mother was in the hospital. After a series of tests, she had received a diagnosis of epilepsy and doctors found a tumor in her brain.

E. Blade's and Harry's Experiences: Stating Their Significance for This Research Undertaking

Together, the stories of these two young men served as reference points for the two types of youth whose interests this book is addressing. In light of his developmental and cognitive differences, Blade represents youth with sociophysiological challenges.

Harry, however, being the U.S.-born son of Haitian immigrants, represents African-Americans. These two young men's stories are woven in the analysis that follows and facilitate an understanding of dis/ability and race in context.

While statistics can be used to make generalizations and persuade, stories have a unique aspect —in the sense that they are more memorable. Presenting Blade's and Harry's stories above fulfills the political involvement mandate, issued by former U.S. President Obama, that I alluded to in this work's introduction. By leaving an imprint in the minds of readers, I hope these stories demonstrate the power of the human element, showing that the injustices facing youth with sociophysiological challenges and of African-American heritage affect real people and not just numbers.

What is more, these two case studies shape the solutions and reforms discussed later on. For instance, because Harry belonged to the Haiti-American subgroup of the broad African-American community, francophone literature is sparsely drawn upon to provide solutions for formerly incarcerated black youth.

While Blade is still alive, Harry is deceased. Harry's death, and the passing of others, should sound the alarm regarding the obstacles that under-served youth face after their incarceration. In analyzing the barriers to community re-entry and describing possible solutions below, I relied on Blade and Harry's stories not only as a source of inspiration but also as a heuristic device: an aid to analysis.

This page left blank intentionally

CHAPTER V

BARRIERS TO RE-INTEGRATION

In this segment of the book, I will first discuss the barriers for youth with sociophysiological challenges, by tackling missed opportunities for screening and tracking and administrative hurdles in the delivery of special education services. Then, I will address the obstacles facing young people of African-American origin, touching upon intergenerational incarceration and issues relating to identity and racial consciousness.

A. Common Barriers

Mutual to formerly incarcerated youth with sociophysiological challenges and of African-American origin are some proverbial barriers. Some of these obstacles constitute difficulties in not continuing with educational careers but also finding a job post-incarceration. In turn, these limitations have spillover effects that affect members of both group in varied ways.

In light of the variation in effects, I outline below some of the hurdles facing youth in both groups. My selection of the issues presented was inspired by the case studies presented above, which outline the experiences of two young men: one with dis/abilities and one who is African-American. The proverbial obstacles facing both group are abundant across the literature. Consequently, I will not focus on what is already well-known and -discussed among scholars. I aim to make distinctive contributions in this work by focusing on issues that relate strictly to the case studies presented, although in a broad sense.

B. Barriers for Youth with Sociophysiological Challenges

i. Screening and Tracking

One of the major issues facing youth with sociophysiological challenges like Blade who have experienced incarceration constitutes receiving special education services when they return to the schools belonging to the communities they are from. Although Blade is still incarcerated, he will face these issues after he gets out, although as an adult —which makes his future case irrelevant here.

In a holistic sense, determining the eligibility of youth formerly facing incarceration for special education services is unfortunately a process fraught with systemic issues. Individual states report a wide variance of in the enrollment of youth in special education post incarceration.[75] Inconsistent systems for labeling and

[75] McDermott, Elana R., Sara Anderson, and Jonathan F. Zaff. "Dropout typologies: Relating profiles of risk and support to lat-

tracking delinquent youth and their non-court or detention-involved counterparts account for part of this variance.

Until the recent past, per federal law, school districts and states did not have to track youth placement into special education, though schools have been tracking special education placement by race, gender, and socio-economic statuses for decades.[76] States now have to compile and report data for youth's enrollment in special education. However, relatively few states have adequate systems for tracking formerly incarcerated juveniles.[77] Tracking is crucial because it affects how lawmakers and school authorities distribute funds for special education and transitional services.

It is additionally problematic that educators and policymakers apply multiple terms with slightly different definitions to youth who are students with dis/abilities.[78] For the large-scale data that do exist, it is difficult to determine whether all youth placements and outcomes are tracked.[79] Schools and other educational entities use the

---

er educational re-engagement." *Applied Developmental Science* (2017): 1-16.

[76] Flynn, Kylie Shawn. "Stability of Special Education Eligibility from Kindergarten to Third Grade." (2017).

[77] *Ibid.*

[78] Spooner, Fred, Bethany R. McKissick, and Victoria F. Knight. "Establishing the state of affairs for evidence-based practices in students with severe disabilities." *Research and Practice for Persons with Severe Disabilities* 42, no. 1 (2017): 8-18.

[79] Nilholm, Claes, and Kerstin Göransson. "What is meant by inclusion? An analysis of European and North American journal articles with high impact." *European Journal of Special Needs Education* (2017): 1-15.

subgroup label SWD's (standing for Students with Dis/abilities) to describe juveniles who lack a number o specified skills, no matter their incarceration experiences.

Once SWD's achieve a satisfactory score on a state proficiency test or meet certain standards in their individualized education plans (IEP's), they lose their SWD designations.[80] This practice and the fact that states largely neglect to keep numerical figures about youth post-incarceration make it difficult to track academic outcomes or data for the supposedly delinquent subgroup —even in districts that consistently use the federal definition or internal labeling and placement o young people with dis/abilities.

A further complicating factor is that many youth, formerly incarcerated, with and without dis/abilities, are also racial minorities or low socio-economic status (SES) students, or both. Blade falls into this category. Racial minority and low SES students have been historically overrepresented in special education.[81] Although youth, formerly-incarcerated, with sociophysiological challenges have not been shown to be consistently overrepresented, they are alternately under- and over-represented at different stages of schooling and across different

[80] Shogren, Karrie A., and Anthony J. Plotner. "Transition planning for students with intellectual disability, autism, or other disabilities: Data from the National Longitudinal Transition Study-2." *Intellectual and developmental disabilities* 50, no. 1 (2012): 16-30.

[81] Shifrer, Dara, Chandra Muller, and Rebecca Callahan. "Disproportionality: A sociological perspective of the identification by schools of students with learning disabilities." In *Disability as a Fluid State*, pp. 279-308. Emerald Group Publishing Limited, 2010.

school systems.[82]

Misidentification of youth for special education carries high stakes for the academic outcomes of students like Blade. Delinquent juveniles who are inappropriately enrolled in special education face a documented risk of detrimental academic effects resulting from the misapplied special education label.[83] Youth who need special education services but are not identified to receive them face compounding learning issues with each year of non-identification.

ii. Administrative Hurdles

Administrative issues at the district, state, and federal levels, along with the inner workings of the school-to-prison pipeline, also contribute to unbalanced representation of youth with sociophysiological challenges in prisons and jails.[84] In some districts, formerly incarcerated juveniles facing physiological challenges can only be designated as part of one at-risk subgroup—they can be labeled as Students with Dis/abilities (SWD's) or delinquent youth, but not both.[85]

[82] Bullis, Michael, and Paul Yovanoff. "More alike than different? Comparison of formerly incarcerated youth with and without disabilities." *Journal of Child and Family Studies* 14, no. 1 (2005): 127-139.

[83] Alltucker, Kevin W., Michael Bullis, Daniel Close, and Paul Yovanoff. "Different pathways to juvenile delinquency: Characteristics of early and late starters in a sample of previously incarcerated youth." *Journal of Child and Family Studies* 15, no. 4 (2006): 475-488.

[84] See, e.g., Barron, Lisa. *The Informed Practice of School Psychology as it Relates to Adjudicated Youth Who Are in Need of Special Education Services*. Alliant International University, 2013.

[85] See, e.g., National Research Council. *Educating one and all: Students with disabilities and standards-based reform*. National

In these districts, delinquent youth enrolled in special education services often lose access to the classes they need because of this either-or form of labelling.[86]

Of greatest concern for formerly incarcerated youth with sociophysiological challenges is ineffective instruction. Nationally, low-quality instruction dominates the in-school hours of youth with sociophysiological challenges.[87] This reality persists in opposition to research indicating that effective and appropriate education in content areas, coupled with socio-emotional instruction, is a more effective model to boost the academic outcomes of youth with sociophysiological challenges who were formerly incarcerated, whether in transition or not.[88]

C. Barriers for African-American Youth

i. Intergenerational Incarceration and Its Implications for African-American Juveniles[89]

American society's relegation of Harry and other

Academies Press, 1997.

[86] *Ibid.*

[87] Wagner, Mary, Krista Kutash, Albert J. Duchnowski, Michael H. Epstein, and W. Carl Sumi. "The children and youth we serve: A national picture of the characteristics of students with emotional disturbances receiving special education." *Journal of emotional and behavioral disorders* 13, no. 2 (2005): 79-96.

[88] Ibid.

[89] This raises the question: Does Parental Incarceration Correlate with Youth Incarceration?

Given the fact that more research is needed to probe the aftershocks of intergenerational incarceration, at this point can scholars even

formerlyincarceratedblackjuvenilestoitsmargins —using partly the prison-industrial complex[90] — is without doubt a multilayered issue. Three years ago, Yale sociologist Christopher Wilderman and Rutgers criminal justice scholar Sarah Wakefield wrote a book[91] explaining why, though they did not address Harry's case in particular. In their

---

pinpoint whether young people with incarcerated parents face a higher risk of ending up in juvenile delinquency facilities? To answer this question, findings from several studies show that parental incarceration can tilt the scale for some young people when it comes to being involved with the youth delinquency system. Through exploring different theory-backed perspectives, researcher Ross Parke outlines various studies that look at developmental and environmental factors contributing to youth incarceration. Parke explores the "parent-child dyad," institutional systems, family networks, and cultural factors —following with a discussion of the short- and long-range consequences of parental incarceration. The key insight arising out of Parke's research revolves around his incarcerated parents' programs summary —concluding that while these parent-adapted intermediation efforts can work, their restricted sample sizes, inadequate follow-up, and inability to methodically pinpoint effective elements of intervention pose significant limitations. Parke, Ross D., and A. Clarke-Stewart. "The effects of parental incarceration on children: Perspectives, promises and policies." *Prisoners once removed* (2003): 189-232. Intervention programs that Parke analyzed encompassed prison visitation programs, rearing children prisons through relying on prison nurseries, and substitutes to incarceration.

[90] The prison-industrial complex is "a complex web of racism, social control, and profit," interweaving "government agencies with business interests that seek to make a profit from imprisoning the poor and people of color." Sudbury, Julia. *Global lockdown: Race, gender, and the prison-industrial complex*. Routledge, 2014 (citing Davis, Angela Y., and Cassandra Shaylor. "Race, gender, and the prison industrial complex: California and beyond." *Meridians* 2, no. 1 (2001): 1-25).

[91] Wakefield, Sara, and Christopher Wildeman. *Children of the prison boom: Mass incarceration and the future of American inequality*. Oxford University Press, 2013.

work, Wakefield and Wilderman tested their hypothesis that intergenerational incarceration heightens inequality, especially for the sons and daughters of incarcerated black fathers.

Using empirical analyses that look at survey data and trends across qualitative interviews, they found support for the idea that mass incarceration has had profoundly harmful consequences on the descendants of those convicted and serving time, particularly African-American juveniles. Some youth cope with a glut of co -existing and -evolving obstacles following their parents' incarceration —including, among others: traumatic separation, stigma, isolation, frequent home and school moves, and low incomes later on in life.[92] These young people tend to also experience compounding traumatic life episodes prior to parental confinement.

Conceivably, formerly black youth, many of whom have incarcerated parents, might be vulnerable to a number of detrimental developmental aftereffects. To analyze this assumption, psychological criminologist and Stockholm Prize in Criminology winner David Farrington and colleagues sifted through empirical evidence concerning correlational and causal links existing between a determinant, i.e., parental incarceration, and four possible aftereffects. These outcomes consisted of: (1) future antisocial behaviors, (2) drug dependence and abuse, (3) educational achievement, and (4) mental health issues.[93] For their meta-analysis,

---

[92] *Ibid.*, p. 46 and 65.

[93] Murray, Joseph, David P. Farrington, and Ivana Sekol. "Children's antisocial behavior, mental health, drug use, and educational

Farrington and his colleagues relied on results from forty studies, with varying sample sizes.

Emerging from Farrington's work are some astounding results. Although these results present a mixed picture, they are worth highlighting to pave the way for future research. The studies with the soundest designs revealed that while parental incarceration connects with a slightly higher risk for antisocial behavior, it has no statistical relationship with mental health troubles, inferior educational achievement, or drug abuse.[94] To be clear, although Farrington's results applied to all youth in general, they can be applied to African-American youth, formerly-incarcerated, as Farrington used a mixed sample size.[95]

ii. Identity and Racial Consciousness

Culture has always been fundamental to both the empowerment and free self-expression of all people, especially young people. For some delinquent black juveniles like Harry, cultural factors can serve as an impediment. The post-

---

performance after parental incarceration: a systematic review and meta-analysis." (2012).

[94] *Ibid.*

[95] Research that controlled for either parents' criminal misconduct or children's antisocial conduct, before parental incarceration, show an added risk of roughly 10% for antisocial behavior between youth with parents behind bars, when contrasted with their peers. (Farrington, *supra*, note 96, p. 106) Despite the statistical strength of their results, these studies had mediocre experimental designs. Therefore, longitudinal analyses that rely on randomized block designs and other experimental techniques that are more precise than the ones used are needed. Rigorous experimental designs would allow researchers to determine with high precision the consequences of intergenerational incarceration.

incarceration obstacles that Harry experienced above had ties to cultural unfitness, particularly his perception that he did not fit within American culture as the son of immigrants.

For centuries, race played a crucial role in marking out cultural difference. The presumption was that each race held a distinct culture that distinguished it from another. Today, Americans from all backgrounds are eager to adopt many aspects of black culture: ranging from hair styles to clothing lines, dance moves and vernacular forms of slang, as well as countless varieties of popular music.[96] Indeed, black cultural attitudes are not only prevalent—they are routinely popularized through concert venues, corporate advertising, and department stores.[97] There are many researchers who believe that cultural differences have narrowed to the point where race has become accidental. This presents some special challenges for formerly incarcerated black youth when attempting to find themselves and reintegrate into their communities and culture.

Columnist Dave Itzkoff makes the argument that blacks, among whom are formerly incarcerated youth, can no longer claim exclusive authority over the direction of their culture. For instance, with respect to hip-hop, an integral part of black culture, Itzkoff thinks that: "It's a slippery slope

---

96 Levine, Lawrence W. *Black culture and black consciousness: Afro-American folk thought from slavery to freedom.* Vol. 530. Oxford University Press, USA, 1978.

97 See, e.g., Neal, Mark Anthony. *What the music said: Black popular music and black public culture. Routledge, 2013; Kitwana, Bakari. Why White Kids Love Hip Hop: Wankstas, Wiggas, Wannabes, and the New Reality of Race in America.* New York: Basic Civitas, 2005: 2.

when you make the argument that hip hop only a black person's art. Certainly its origins are in that community, but if you want hip-hop to endure. . . you have to let other people have their way with it."[98] This form of cultural upheaval can spell trouble for some youth who may find it harder than it would have otherwise been to reintegrate in their communities. This was particularly Harry's experience as he was an amateur hip hop artist, with a professionally-produced album, pre-incarceration.[99]

Incateringtomostlywhitesuburbanites,America's mainstream has been willing to fetishize black culture as a commodity for mass consumption. Yet these manifestations of culture are seldom if ever interested in depicting the daily experience of African-Americans, for many of whom culture has been a way of life. Nor do they seem geared towards the betterment of that community, which continues to endure unacceptable levels of marginalization and institutional racism. What this shows is that despite the appearance of assimilation, America's mainstream still remains committed to the logic of race. Even as it indulges and bears out every gratification imaginable, it is still hesitant to accept a deeper expression of blackness. Formerly incarcerated black youth seeking to reenter their communities struggle

[98] Neal, *supra*, note 100, p. 23.

[99] Of course, few would disagree with Itzkoff that many whites enjoy black culture. Yet formerly incarcerated black youth must ask themselves why Americans continue to encounter so few expressions of black artistry, which can make black youth feel out of place in American society. Even as Black culture has achieved a normative presence in the mainstream, the extent to which the black experience is seen and heard is quite elusive.

with the act of defining their culture and, in turn, their identity.

CHAPTER VI

SOLUTIONS

In this section, I look at societal re-integration, at professional and social levels, for youth, formerly-incarcerated, with sociophysiological challenges. For this camp, I will address social reintegration before focusing more specifically on returns to professional activity. These socially- and professionally-oriented solutions aim to counter the obstacles that youth have encountered in their efforts to socialize and restart their professional careers post-incarceration. I opted to proffer social and professional solutions because while virtually all youth will have to socialize and work to make a living post incarceration, some of them decide to abandon their educational paths, in light of the systemic obstacles that have thwarted their educational progress. Human beings are undoubtedly social animals. Finally, troubleshooting and proposing solutions for educational obstacles would be less effective, as the causal factors for lack of educational progress are convoluted and difficult to pinpoint.

Concerning youth, formerly incarcerated, and of Black heritage, I provide solution measures addressing intergenerational incarceration and issues of identity development. These measures, corresponding with the obstacles raised above, implicitly incorporate the second case study, by seeking to highlight Harry's quasi-artistic interest in applying critical literary concepts towards political ends that are substantively transcendental.

A. Solutions for Youth with Sociophysiological Challenges

i. Reintegration

1. *Social Skills Development*

Social insertion, or reintegration, as opposed to exclusion, constitutes the creation and maintenance of relationships with others —forming the basis for belonging to a community. The degree of social integration is defined, on the one hand, by the quality and frequency of the relationships established with the members of a particular communal group; and, on the other, by individuals' respective sense of belonging towards their communities. A group is integrated when its members feel connected to one another by shared values, common goals, and the feeling of taking part in a collective constantly reinforced by regular interactions.[100] If the process of exclusion is multifaceted, the process of insertion must be multidimensional and take into account the social needs of the persons affected.

Based on the above definition of social integration, it can be seen that juvenile

---

[100] Berkman, Lisa F., Thomas Glass, Ian Brissette, and Teresa E. Seeman. "From social integration to health: Durkheim in the new millennium." *Social science & medicine* 51, no. 6 (2000): 843-857.

delinquent youth with sociophysiological challenges, while incarcerated, can easily be integrated into their penal communities. It is possible, though difficult, or youth to maintain a degree of connection with other inmates and guards. Moreover, it is easy to suppose that a group of prisoners can share common desires and dreams —which is a factor of integration.

However, post-incarceration, youth, formerly-incarcerated and grappling with sociophysiological challenges, confront the fact that they are excluded by the criminal records that follow them, but also because of the prejudices held by the society.[101] States should put in place programs that allow youth to establish good relationships, knowledge of the rules of acceptable social conducts, and the capacity to adapt to environments by understanding social cues.

For youth, formerly incarcerated, who are often highly marginalized, it is possible they may have some gaps in social skills.[102] Programs designed by practitioners with expertise in this area, such as psychiatrists, therapists, and social workers, can aid with the sharpening of social skills.

---

[101] Hirschfield, Paul J. "The Declining Significance of Delinquent Labels in Disadvantaged Urban Communities1." In *Sociological Forum*, vol. 23, no. 3, pp. 575-601. Blackwell Publishing Ltd, 2008.

[102] Rohde, Paul, Jenel S. Jorgensen, John R. Seeley, and David E. Mace. "Pilot evaluation of the coping course: A cognitive-behavioral intervention to enhance coping skills in incarcerated youth." *Journal of the American Academy of Child & Adolescent Psychiatry* 43, no. 6 (2004): 669-676.

2. Professional Skills Training

In a society fundamentally structured around economic roles, the most integrating continuum along which community re-integration takes place is labor. According to Freud, work is the strongest link between "man and reality."[103] Although this quote dates back to the nineteenth century, it is valid today, as Americans are very oten defined by their professional activities.

Contemporary professional careers entail more than simply working. At their core, they constitute maintaining professional relationships and engaging in spaces whose potential for social ties is important. For most people, a job is a form of belonging and a means through which one can define her/his financial and social standing.

States should put in place programs that allow youth, formerly incarcerated, with sociophysiological challenges to engage in professional activities that nourish their professional ambitions. The proverbial work training programs would be useful in this realm.[104] Such job programs would not only allow youth to build their résumés, they would also help them to create professional relationships that would help them obtain employment in their future.

---

[103] Jones, Ernest. "Sigmund Freud, Life and Work. Vol. 3: The Last Phase." (1959).

[104] Bullis, Michael, Paul Yovanoff, and Emily Havel. "The importance of getting started right: Further examination of the facility-to-community transition of formerly incarcerated youth." *The Journal of Special Education* 38, no. 2 (2004): 80-94.

The literature regarding this topic is scarce on details regarding what such programs would entail. From personal experience, when I volunteered at Access Living, I saw some young people facing sociophysiological challenges who benefitted from programming that taught them a number of skills that allowed them to obtain employment at partner organizations. For youth with sociophysiological challenges who have criminal records, finding work can be tremendously difficult. Programs such as this would ease community reentry for these young people.

B. Solutions for African-American Youth Regarding Issues of Identity and Racial Consciousness

i. <u>Countering the Aftereffects of Intergenerational Incarceration</u>

For black youth, formerly-incarcerated, in transition, many exploratory examples to counter intergenerational incarceration abound. While residing in Paris, prominent black figures such as Aimé Césaire and Léon Damas were marginalized in their repeated attempts to be included within French society. Yet in experiencing this rejection, these men were inspired to assert their own racial identities, using the subjective voice of poetry to rehabilitate their "blackness." Although Césaire and Damas were adults, there is much that young people can learn from the challenges they encountered. In many ways, Césaire's and Damas's creative efforts preceded the works of Paulette Nardal, who was among the first to explore representations of black consciousness.

By examining the expressions of Césaire and Damas, and the pioneering work of Paulette Nardal, black youth in transition would gain an understanding of black consciousness in its full depth. In doing so, they would come to a better understanding of their identity. Such an understanding would help in overcoming the effects on intergenerational incarceration by empowering black youth.

Through an application of Intersectional Theory,[105] it can be postulated that marginalized persons have a lot to learn from one another — particularly when put to the test.[106] Black juveniles, in seeking to transition back into society post-incarceration, face a crucial test which calls for an awareness of identity and socio-economic positioning.

Racial awareness, particularly in its provision of a collective sense of identity, would solve some of the problems associated with intergenerational incarceration, as it could engender social revolt. Many black juveniles have explained how they lack role models to whom they can look for models of achievement.[107] Acquiring inspirations from black adults who have reached

---

[105] See, e.g., Lykke, Nina. Feminist studies: A guide to intersectional theory, methodology and writing. Routledge, 2010.

[106] O'Sullivan, Edmund. "Transformative learning." *Educational Vision for the* 2, no. 1 (1999).

[107] Assibey-Mensah, George O. "Role models and youth development: Evidence and lessons from the perceptions of African-American male youth." *The Western Journal of Black Studies* 21, no. 4 (1997): 242.

great heights could provide useful examples.

ii. Identity Development

The literary works that were part of the Harlem Renaissance, of the 1930's, in the United States helped to create a new consciousness amongst blacks. This literary movement and other notable black-led intellectual movements throughout American history can inspire young people, if they are restructured to cater to the needs of black youth who were formerly incarcerated.

During the twentieth century, the moment had come to unveil the authenticity and existential richness o "black consciousness" —a project that was first realized through the reflections o Paulette Nardal.[108] Juvenile delinquent youth can follow in Nardal's footsteps.

Being predominantly black, juvenile delinquent youth, with and without dis/abilities, can spread messages about their communities in the pursuit o comparable ends. In a different context, while living in Martinique, Paulette and her sister hosted Sunday meetings which contained a library of Francophone and African-American works, for her peers.[109] If transitional programs for juvenile delinquent youth were to, for instance, create centers that would allow black juveniles to engage in a similar pursuit, these

108 Sharpley-Whiting, Tracy Denean. "Paulette Nardal, Race Consciousness, and Antillean Letters." *The Quest for Community and Identity: Critical Essays in Africana Social Philosophy* (2002): 143.

109 Wilder, Gary. The French Imperial Nation-state: Negritude & Colonial Humanism between the Two World Wars. Chicago: University of Chicago, 2005: 174

young people would achieve greater success of reintegrating into society.[110]

[110] In seeking to effectuate change within the transitional experiences of formerly incarcerated youth with sociophysiological challenges, Langston Hughes' writings are particularly compelling. It can spark within delinquent youth a desire to want to understand black culture in all its dimensions, and how that culture could affect their emotional, social, and artistic integrity as black and brown human beings. Upon reading Langton's writings, juvenile delinquents can learn about the many ways in which black culture has informed their own consciousness, and how that culture has always signified a kind of identity for them.

CHAPTER VII

EASING YOUTH TRANSITIONS THROUGH LEGAL REFORM AVENUES

There are three persistent tensions that complicate the reforming of measures capable of improving the community reentry experiences for youth with sociophysiological challenges and of African-American origin. One, practices at juvenile delinquency facilities are continuously changing. Second, there is the challenge of developing incarceration alternatives that have the capacity of making communities safe without expanding the size of the so-called penal state —i.e., lawyers and judges, law enforcement personnel, prison officials, and other institutions that work together to incarcerate youth. Finally, there is the need to tackle interpersonal violence while putting front and center the interests of youth with sociophysiological challenges and of African-American origin.

In this section, I will cover a limited number of reform measures designed to benefit formerly incarcerated youth with sociophysiological challenges and African-American juveniles. Thereafter, I will describe a number of measures that are not particular fitted to either group, intended to benefit members of both group and beyond.

A. Youth with Sociophysiological Challenges

i. Preclude the Sidestepping of Special Education Protections.

Federal law mandates that schools educate formerly incarcerated young people with dis/abilities in classrooms that allow them to learn alongside their peers who do not have dis/abilities, to the greatest appropriate extent. Sometimes, however, school systems shortchange these young people through offering them an education that is not in keeping with the provisions of relevant state and federal laws —leading these students to make deficient progress in their educational careers and later on their professions. For juveniles with dis/abilities who have faced incarceration, educational achievement can be marginal, and in some cases, totally off-limits. This is true although federal law guarantees these young individuals a "free and appropriate education" until the age of twenty-one, as explained below.

Through one of its subsections, i.e., Part B, the Individuals with Disabilities Education Act (IDEA), a law that Congress enacted in 1990, places legal limits on the actions of state education agencies and nonprofit organizations in educating these juveniles.[111] Among the organizational

[111] United States Department of Education. Office of Special Education and Rehabilitative Services. December 5, 2014. Accessed May 12, 2017. https://www2.ed.gov/policy/gen/guid/correctional-education/idea-letter.pdf.

entities affected are prisons and detention centers. According to the U.S. Department of Education, "Absent a specific exception, all IDEA protections apply to youth who are students with disabilities in correctional facilities and their parents."[112] Youth with sociophysiological challenges in delinquency facilities receive protection from two other Federal laws: Section 504 of the Rehabilitation Act of 1973, outlawing dis/ability discrimination in programs of entities accepting federal financial assistance;[113] and Title II of the Americans with Disabilities Act of 1990, banning dis/ability discrimination by public entities, such as public schools and juvenile delinquency facilities, even if they do not rely on federal financial assistance.[114]

The Department buttresses this claim by explaining that backing the provision of first-rate education for vulnerable youth can benefit American society socioeconomically in many ways. The act of helping struggling youth in their pursuit of educational achievement contributes toward the enrichment of these individuals' future employment and life prospects. Students' past, or current, incarceration does, in no way, rid them of the substantive rights and procedural safeguards and remedies that the IDEA affords students with dis/abilities and their legal guardians. The Department of Education should pursue enforcement rules enforcement programs to ensure that special education protections are not sidestepped.

---

[112] *Ibid.*, p. 1.

[113] 29 U.S.C. §794, 34 CFR part 104.

[114] 42 U.S.C. §§12131-12134, 28 CFR part 35.

B. African-American Youth

i. Tackle Disproportions in Juvenile Delinquency Referrals That Are Directly Race-Based.

Lawyers and other advocates working to deal with racial gaps in the juvenile delinquency system ought to consider the likelihood of relying on the Juvenile Justice and Delinquency Prevention Act (JJDPA) of 1974, a federal law through which states that follow a number of federal protections can obtain funding for the care and treatment of youth in the juvenile delinquency system.115

At present, this Act does not allow for a private right of action, or an alternative significant enforcement means.[116] Nevertheless, the Act persists as a critical device to ceding access to information regarding disproportionate minority representation[117] —in light of the fact that data can be relied upon to buttress system-level racial discrimination claims.

---

[115] P.L. 93-415, 42 U.S.C. 5601 *et seq*.

[116] Tulman, Joseph B., and Douglas M. Weck. "Shutting off the school-to-prison pipeline for status offenders with education-related disabilities." *NYL Sch. L. Rev*. 54 (2009): 875; Gonzalez, Thalia. "Keeping kids in schools: Restorative justice, punitive discipline, and the school to prison pipeline." *JL & Educ*. 41 (2012): 281.

[117] Huizinga, David, Terrence Thornberry, Kelly Knight, Peter Lovegrove, Rolf Loeber, Karl Hill, and David P. Farrington. "Disproportionate minority contact in the juvenile justice system: A study of differential minority arrest/referral to court in three cities." *Washington, DC: Office of Juvenile Justice and Delinquency Prevention* (2007).

C. General Reform Measures

i. Remove the Incentives for Youth to Offend in the First Place.

Countless young men and women who end up behind bars have experiences with adults and professionals neglecting their psychosocial needs and society disregarding, in part or whole, their socioeconomic well-being. If effective prevention or early intervention were to be afforded to even 10% of young offenders, millions of dollars spent towards incarceration could be saved annually. Although institutional investment in prevention and early intervention has increased somewhat in the past decades,118 pressures to produce outcomes in the short-term often chips away at that investment. Focused and well-governed prevention and early intervention programs can be fruitful if they are well-coordinated at the nation-wide and local levels.

Mainstream institutions, encompassing primary and secondary schools and health services organizations, ought to increase their involvement in warding off *violent* youth offending —through experimenting with different prevention and intervention models, among which are the social development model put forth by Endowed Professor in Prevention, J. David Hawkins, and criminologist Joseph Weis.[119]

[118] Meisels, Samuel J., and Jack P. Shonkoff. "Early childhood intervention: A continuing evolution." *Handbook of early childhood intervention* 2 (2000): 3-31.

[119] Hawkins, J. David, and Joseph G. Weis. "The social development model: An integrated approach to delinquency prevention." *The Journal of Primary Prevention* 6, no. 2 (1985): 73-97.

ii. Concentrate on Violent Youth Recidivists.

Although violent youth recidivists worry Americans most, too many status offences reach the courts.[120] To claim more court time and resources that court personnel and social support organizations can use to address and prevent the actions of repeated and violent youth offenders, states and communities should address status offences outside of courts, using restorative justice practices.[121]

In some ways, some communities and jurisdictions already apply this recommendation through relying on youth diversion programs — alternatives to formal processing of youth in the juvenile delinquency system.[122] These programs aim to redirect young offenders from the juvenile delinquency system through planning, supervision, and furnishing social supports. In a reform vein, more jurisdictions need to adopt the youth diversion model for status offenses while referring youthful offenders at risk of committing violence to youth offender panels. Referrals, in this context, would be for fixed periods of time and courts would have the authority to systematically

---

[120] Barrett, David E., Antonis Katsiyannis, and Dalun Zhang. "Predictors of offense severity, prosecution, incarceration and repeat violations for adolescent male and female offenders." *Journal of Child and Family Studies* 15, no. 6 (2006): 708-718.

[121] Bonta, James, Suzanne Wallace-Capretta, Jennifer Rooney, and Kevin Mcanoy. "An outcome evaluation of a restorative justice alternative to incarceration." *Contemporary Justice Review* 5, no. 4 (2002): 319-338.

[122] Wilson, Holly A., and Robert D. Hoge. "The effect of youth diversion programs on recidivism: A meta-analytic review." *Criminal Justice and Behavior* 40, no. 5 (2013): 497-518.

re-examine peculiar cases, changing sentences to deal with egregious circumstances.

iii. Make Youth Rehabilitation More Cost-Effective and Transparent.

Some sentences lead to improved outcomes and are literally less expensive than others, in terms of the fees affiliated with them.[123] Custody is the priciest, yet among the least effective, sentences.[124] Some jurisdictions have introduced intensive supervision probation programs (ISPP's) to strengthen community-based incarceration alternatives and keep recidivist youthful offenders in their homes and in school and training or job programs.[125] The majority of recidivist youthful offenders who might otherwise end up behind bars ought to receive placement in an ISPP instead.[126] Contemporary efforts to cut commitments to incarceration must accentuate the need to: raise judges' confidence in community-based programs; give more feedback to high-incarceration areas regarding the costs,

---

[123] Olson, David E., and Gerard F. Ramker. "Crime does not pay, but criminals may: Factors influencing the imposition and collection of probation fees." *The Justice System Journal* (2001): 29-46.

[124] Broadhurst, Roderic G., and Ross A. Mailer. "The recidivism of prisoners released for the first time: Reconsidering the effectiveness question." *Australian & New Zealand Journal of Criminology* 23, no. 2 (1990): 88-104.

[125] Paparozzi, Mario A., and Paul Gendreau. "An intensive supervision program that worked: Service delivery, professional orientation, and organizational supportiveness." *The Prison Journal* 85, no. 4 (2005): 445-466.

[126] Petersilia, Joan, and Susan Turner. "Evaluating Intensive Supervision Probation/Parole: Results of a Nationwide Experilllent." (1993).

monetary and otherwise, and the efficacy of community-based custody alternatives; and raise public awareness concerning youth criminality and the results of incarcerating delinquent juveniles.

iv. Make Changes to the Juvenile Delinquency Laws in Order to Prevent the Sharing of Juvenile Records with the General Public and Enact Thorough Sealing Definitions.

Some state laws permit liberal sharing of juvenile delinquency records —at times sanctioning public disclosures.[127] With the expansion of legal sharing limits, the risk of detrimental and unlawful information release regarding formerly incarcerated youth who are trying to reintegrate back into society heightens. Access to juvenile delinquency records should be restricted to parties possessing an indispensable need for criminality-related information. To achieve this objective, states ought to get rid of any statutory provisions that give members of the general public rights to youth delinquency information.

For additional guarding and simplicity vis-à-vis juvenile delinquency records, legislators should change pertinent laws (e.g., Illinois's Juvenile Court Act) to insert comprehensive sealing definitions to their confidentiality provisions.[128]

---

[127] Blankley, Kristen M. "Are Public Records Too Public-Why Personally Identifying Information Should Be Removed from Both Online and Print Versions of Court Documents." *Ohio St. LJ* 65 (2004): 413.

[128] Gough, Aidan R. "The Expungement of Adjudication Records of Juvenile and Adult Offenders: A Problem of Status." *Wash. ULQ*

These definitions have to spell out that juvenile delinquency records are sealed except in case where legal provisions outright maintain otherwise and stay sealed when youth offenders become adults. These definitions should also provide that sealed records cannot be divulged outside of the confines that laws specifically carve out; and that these records ought to be disclosed only with the juvenile courts' approval, once petitioners have demonstrated good cause establishing that their use is necessary.

v. Plug the Gaps that Leave Out Juvenile Delinquency Records from the Confidentiality Provisions that State Laws Guarantee.

The confidentiality protections embedded in pertinent state laws ought to apply to records that document violations of municipal ordinances, laws that local governments enact. This minor change would plug loopholes that render millions of juvenile records accessible to the public, comprising employers, educational institutions, and prospective land -lords and –ladies (property owners).

Furthermore, all states ought to put in place a means to remove juvenile delinquency records from Federal Bureau of Investigation (FBI) databanks.[129] Millions of juvenile delinquency records are stored on FBI databases accessible

(1966): 147.

[129] Jacobs, James, and Tamara Crepet. "The expanding scope, use, and availability of criminal records." *NYUJ Legis. & Pub. Pol'y* 11 (2007): 177.

to select organizational entities.[130] Most of these delinquency records emerged after the commission of nonviolent offenses and many were borne out of arrests that never made it to court.[131]

FBI records do not differentiate among adult and juvenile crimes. What is worse, record-closure facts —e.g., information regarding arrests that did not lead to charges —seldom register on FBI databases. Faced with these limited data points, hiring entities and other parties might make the most adverse assumptions: that information FBI records reveal adult convictions. Eliminating these juvenile delinquency records from the FBI databanks would offer relief for millions of young men and women. As such, a mechanism to achieve this ought to be designed and put into practice instantly.

vi. Exact Penalties and Establish Causes of Action for Illegal Disclosure of Juvenile Delinquency Records.

Short of legal penalties for unlawful disclosure of juvenile delinquency information, organizations have nearly no motivation to abide by the confidentiality protections carved in relevant state laws. In keeping with the efforts of 16 states and the Model Act Governing the Confidentiality and Expungement of Juvenile Delinquency Records (hereinafter the Model Act), devised by the American Bar Association (ABA), 34 states

---

[130] Jacobs, James, and Tamara Crepet. "The expanding scope, use, and availability of criminal records." *NYUJ Legis. & Pub. Pol'y* 11 (2007): 177.

[131] *Ibid.*

should impose sanctions for illicit record sharing, classifying this activity as a misdemeanor and enforcing the imposition of a fine.[132] Furthermore, all states should invent a cause of action that can be pursued in civil court to permit injured individuals to claim and recover damages from individuals or institutions that criminally unveil confidential information. These provisions would provide some remedy for individuals whom prohibited sharing has harmed and would discourage sharing.

vii. Get Rid of Fees that States Charge for Expungement.

Youth who have experienced the juvenile delinquency system largely come from underprivileged backgrounds. In consequence, fees may serve as a major expungement stumbling block.[133] Juvenile expungement expenses, reaching hundreds of dollars even for young people who never even faced criminal charges, can prove difficult to afford —given the lack of jobs for youth with a juvenile record.

In some jurisdictions, although fee waivers exist, people who most need them often do not get them.[134] Despite the low affordability of, and other

[132] Illinois Juvenile Justice Commision. "Burdened for Life: The Myth of Juvenile Record Confidentiality and Expungement in Illinois." Accessed May 12, 2017. http://www.law.northwestern.edu/legalclinic/cfjc/documents/Commission-Report-4-27-16-web.pdf.

[133] Shlosberg, Amy, Evan J. Mandery, Valerie West, and Bennett Callaghan. "Expungement and post-exoneration offending." *J. Crim. L. & Criminology* 104 (2014): 353.

[134] Litwok, Daniel. "Have You Ever Been Convicted of a Crime? The Effects of Juvenile Expungement on Crime, Educational, and Labor

issues associated with, these fees, the revenue that governmental agencies receive from such fees is tiny. Restructuring the expungement process could increase these revenues.[135] Drawing on the ABA's recommendations that 17 states have adopted to prohibit charging and expungement fees, all remaining 33 states should get rid of expenses linked to the expungement process for youth.[136]

viii. Educate Law Enforcement Agencies and Clerk's Offices About How They Can Improve Their Compliance with Juvenile Expungement Laws.

Court clerks along with law enforcement personnel in charge of superintending expungement processes for youth too often have little idea regarding state expungement laws or the duties that legislators statutorily impose upon them.[137] They frequently neglect to apprise young men and women of the expungement possibilities and sometimes disseminating myths among youth.[138] Institutional entities with law enforcement mandates and court clerk's offices

---

Market Outcomes." *Unpublished doctoral dissertation). Michigan State University, East Lansing* (2014).

[135] Roberts, Jenny. "Expunging America's Rap Sheet in the Information Age." (2015).

[136] Pager, Devah. "Evidence-Based Policy for Successful Prisoner Reentry." *Criminology & Public Policy* 5, no. 3 (2006): 505-514.

[137] Myrick, Amy. "Facing your criminal record: Expungement and the collateral problem of wrongfully represented self." *Law & Society Review* 47, no. 1 (2013): 73-104.

[138] Sholsberg, Amy, Evan Mandery, and Valerie West. "The expungement myth." *Alb. L. Rev.* 75 (2011): 1229.

ought to receive additional training and education regarding the juvenile expungement process.[139] This would deepen youth's comprehension of these issues and facilitate compliance with their duties. Such educational, or training, programs should stress the procedural steps required to successfully seek expungement and point out the benefits of expungement.

[139] Franklin, Marc A., and Diane Johnsen. "Expunging criminal records: Concealment and dishonesty in an open society." *Hofstra L. Rev.* 9 (1980): 733.

This page left blank intentionally

CHAPTER VIII

CONCLUSION

To ensure the effectuation of fruitful rehabilitation and societal reintegration efforts, consideration of the needs of young people with sociophysiological challenges, not solely youth with sociophysiological challenges and those of African-American origin, must be front and center. Most, if not all, young people who enter juvenile delinquency facilities possess a varied mix of needs: broadly falling in the realms of education, socialization, and professional training. Academics have documented the elevated rates of behavioral and learning disorders among incarcerated youth since at least the 1990's.[140] The common suffering from such disorders among youth behind bars has aptly pushed some academics to equate juvenile delinquency facilities to a default path for some youth with sociophysiological challenges and have encountered failure in schools.[141] While the incarceration

[140] Moffitt, T. E. (1990). Juvenile Delinquency and Attention Deficit Disorder: Boys' Developmental Trajectories from Age 3 to Age 15. *Child Development*, 61, 893-910.

[141] Nelson, C. M. (2000). Educating Students with Emotional and Behavioral Disabilities in the 21st Century: Looking Through

rates for all youth have gone down in the past decade, the percentage of black youth in jails and prisons has increased —raising questions of fairness and whether bias clouds the way in which America punishes those who have violated its laws.

A number of academics have traced the high proportion of youth with sociophysiological challenges and of African-American origin confined in America's correctional facilities.[142] What is more, the empirical findings of a meta-analytical study conducted by the Urban Institute confirm what numerous critics of America's criminal justice system already suspected and this work previously discussed —viz., that most people serving time in American jails and prisons, young and old, suffer from behavioral health issues and/or members of racial minority groups.

Failure to account for sociophysiological challenges and ensure that justice is bias-free —in and outside of juvenile delinquency facilities —foments the cyclical relationship existing between juvenile crimes and recidivism. Every year, through arrests, the country's criminal justice system claims at least 9% of young men, aged between 10 to 17 years.[143] More pressing is the fact that, at a minimum, one in three of the young people arrested and incarcerated faces a sociophysiological

---

Windows, Opening Doors. *Education and Treatment of Children*, 23, 204 – 222.

[142] Christle, Christine A., Kristine Jolivette, and C. Michael Nelson. "Breaking the school to prison pipeline: Identifying school risk and protective factors for youth delinquency." *Exceptionality* 13, no. 2 (2005): 69-88.

[143] In many metropolitan areas, e.g., Chicago, the rate is likely higher. See Office of Juvenile Justice and Delinquency Prevention. "OJJDP Statistical Briefing Book." Washington, DC: U.S. Department of Justice (2009). Accessed May 12, 2017 (http://www.ojjdp.gov/ ojstatbb/crime/JAR_Display.asp?ID=qa05230).

challenge —encompassing emotional dis/ability, learning difficulties, and other conditions.[144] Similarly, as reported earlier, roughly a third of arrests comprise African-American youth. When young men and women end up behind bars, some stay there and become adult inmates, while others get out after long and short sentences and seek to start new lives.

This work addressed some of the challenges that formerly incarcerated youth have faced —analyzing a host of issues that relate to transitioning from juvenile facilities to general society. I offered countless solution and reform measures capable of easing youth's transitions. Before that, I introduced this work's chief focus, outlined the methodology along which it would proceed, reviewed relevant parts of the literary landscape, provided background information that comprises a number of case studies, and reviewed a limited number of barriers to reintegration. Future research should go towards using quantitative methods to evaluate the merits of my recommendations.

[144] Quinn, Mary Magee, Robert B. Rutherford, Peter E. Leone, David M. Osher, and Jeffrey M. Poirier. "Youth with disabilities in juvenile corrections: A national survey." *Exceptional children* 71, no. 3 (2005): 339-345.

This page left blank intentionally

APPENDICES

This page left blank intentionally

TRANSPARENT PEER REVIEW REPORTS

This page left blank intentionally

Peer Review Report of Attorney Mariane Trevisan

i. Introduction

First of all, I would like to introduce myself as an expert on the subject. My name is Mariane Trevisan, I am a Bachelor of Laws and a Lawyer, specialized in International Law by the Brazilian Law School, with professional experience and several articles published on Human Rights and International Law. During my undergraduate studies I worked in several public agencies, the most relevant for this research was my internship at the Public Defender's Office of the State of São Paulo, where I worked as a trainee in Criminal Enforcement. Furthermore, in 2022 I had an article about Human Rights approved and presented at the Universidad Complutense in Madrid, in Spain. I am fluent in Portuguese and English, and Spanish and French at advanced levels.

The present project demonstrates its pertinence already in the title, arousing latent curiosity in the reader about the conclusions made. The relevance of the theme is to analyze the incarceration of young people from another perspective: from a social and humanitarian point of view, focusing on the problems faced by young people with socio-physiological disabilities (not only in the sense of disability in the strict sense) and by young people from African-American communities.

Here I will open a parenthesis to commend the author for using the correct nomenclature for people with disabilities, as defined by the United Nations Convention on the Rights of Persons with Disabilities, which was approved by the UN General Assembly on December 13, 2006[145]. It may seem simple or trivial to use the correct nomenclature, but it is not. This process of recognizing and correctly naming a group of people who are marginalized minorities in society recognizes and reinforces the basic principle of international human rights law, which is the dignity of the human person, and helps to place them on an equal footing with all other citizens as subjects of rights in a society.

The peer-to-peer review that I am writing will be based on two main aspects: (1) the substance of the work, making some notes on possible improvements that would help give the project a greater scientific and legal basis and (2) the quality of its translation from English to French.

ii. Development

The important points of the text and that deserve due appreciation, besides the humanitarian vision followed, is the emotion in the narrative employed by the author, being one of the most

[145]Available in https://www.unicef.org/brazil/convencao-sobre-os-direitos-das-pessoas-com-deficiencia.

important linguistic points. The author uses data and statistics to demonstrate to the reader how the gap occurs in the post-prison reinsertion of young people with disabilities and young people from the American black community. In addition, he uses a personal story from a close friend to demonstrate the statistics and give the numbers a name and a face. This allows the reader to get closer to the statistics and to identify with them.

This allows an approximation with the reader and a greater identification, provoking the thought that such injustices could happen to the reader himself or to any person near and dear to him, being inevitable not to reflect on the theme and not to pay attention to the relevance of its discussion.

The Project is important to shed light on the human rights of people who often are not seen by the system of a country, which is the case of black and/or disabled youth who have been incarcerated, and who have the right to return to their routine life and achieve their personal and professional success after prison. It is not about judging the crime committed, it is about guaranteeing the existential minimum to ensure the rights and citizenship of people deprived of liberty, because they are citizens as much as any other person in America, and this has been duly, statistically and legally substantiated by the author.

The summary was direct and brings the objectives and the dialectic used by the author, in which he points out the main theme and reveals, briefly, some of the challenges faced, as well as the steps followed in conducting the study. It also bases the theme on case study evidence faced by the author as a lawyer defending young African-American men.

The preface addresses the research, who would be interested in reading and knowing about the subject studied: "people who think highly of racial justice and human rights but who, for untold reasons, do not yet grasp the depth and seriousness of the obstacles facing youth with sociophysiological challenges, particularly those who have been incarcerated", in the author's words. This addressing is important to cause a certain critical provocation in the reader. The human rights advocate and person concerned with racial justice may find themselves puzzled and questioned that they may never have thought about the biases of post incarceration life for African American people and people with disabilities.

The introduction begins with a quote from Nelson Mandela, former president of South Africa and an important exponent in the racial struggle worldwide, which brings a scholarship to the text, supporting the emotional bias brought later by the author with the identification of the case experienced by his personal friend. I would cite in the introduction, as well as in the abstract, the methodologies adopted, in a brief way, since they will be discussed in a separate chapter, but only to situate the reader, since he may not have paid attention to these observations in the abstract, just for technical reasons.

iii. Methodology

As for the adoption and explanation of the methodologies used, the observations made were very well clarified and detailed, with a critical eye, exposing to the reader that the law and the legislators need to pay attention to the social context, and not only adopt a solely positivist bias, in which the changes and the fateful situations of society are not taken into account, as observed in the present project. According to the author, the problem of the vulnerability of young people, especially young people serving sentences and who are African-American and/or disabled, in the reinsertion to life in society after prison is not observed. The author sees that there is no free society if people and the law do not pay attention to its future: the young people.

Regarding the above paragraph, I would like to make a sociological and criminological approach. Based on the positivist criminological doctrine, which has Cesare Lombroso as one of its main exponents, the delinquent is classified according to an anthropological view, in which the physiognomic characteristics of the perpetrator of a crime are what would determine whether or not that person has the profile of a criminal. Therefore, the weight, the hair, the size of the skull, the size of the legs, among other characteristics, according to Lombroso, were what would show that the agent had or not the determinism for crime, i.e., the person who commits any type of crime would be a "born" criminal, with biological characteristics that would determine this. It would not take into consideration any other causes that could contribute to the commission of a crime, such as environmental and social variables.

I cite such an approach to draw a parallel with the non-valuation of young people in society, especially young people who are on the margins of society, which here in this project are African-Americans and people with disabilities. Perhaps the legislation and society as a whole do not see these young people due to a reinforcement of the stereotype of "a criminal profile", biased in a historical prejudice coming from the dominant classes with black people, for example, and that for many people, they would not even be subjects worthy of state protection, even more young black people who have committed some type of criminal offense.

Furthermore, the author brings several contextualizations, pointing out several sides of the analysis of the theme, which allows the reader to deepen the details of the subject.

iv. Literature

The author pointed out points of view of different doctrines on the subject, including a criticism on the lack of studies on the subject brought by him in the literature. I make a point that I considered very important, which is: "In the recent past, academics who subscribe to the tenets of cultural criminology and labeling theory have held that the markers assigned to individuals, such as "criminal," might contribute to increases in marginalization and the number of crimes that youth commit. Some theorists have suggested, convincingly, that poverty and inequality have limited youth's access to opportunities. For young people, inadequate practices in the realm of parenting, poor socialization skills, peer pressure, and economic ups and downs in the form of income shocks have led to a "drifting" between conventional mores and delinquency", in the words of the author.

I believe that the author could have brought to support his point here a thought from criminal sociology and modern criminology concerning the consensus schools and the conflict schools. I highlight in the first school the Chicago School doctrine, which brings the Ecological or Social Disorganization Theory, coined by Clifford Shaw and Henry McKay, in which, in a very succinct manner, it explains that due to the disorderly growth of the city of Chicago, This theory, coined by Clifford Shaw and Henry McKay, explains that due to the disorderly growth of the city of Chicago, which expanded from the center to the outskirts (singular centrifugal movement), numerous and serious social, economic, cultural and other problems have created a favorable environment for the installation of crime, aggravated by the absence of mechanisms of social control coined by the absence of the State in these places. This theory also brings a stamp of determinism in the analysis of criminality based on each one of the zones of the city, which does not take into consideration crimes committed by people from the dominant classes (such as white collar crimes), reinforcing once more the stereotype of the peripheral youngster, often black, as a criminal.

Regarding what I consider to be the most important doctrine to support the author's point of view, which is the doctrine of Labelling Abroach (or Symbolic Interactionism/Labeling/Labeling or Social Reaction), the most famous Conflict Theory, coined by Erving Goffman and Howard Becker. According to this doctrine, it is based on the fact that agents who have committed deviant behavior (classified as criminal) are subjected to a ritualized and stigmatizing response (prison), which causes social distancing and reduced opportunities (stigmatization), leading to the emergence of a delinquent subculture with repercussions on self-image. Even after leaving prison, the offender suffers the stigma resulting from institutionalization, and often reoffends. Here lies the crux of the question raised by the author, in would it be possible to base oneself on this theory to give doctrinal foundation to the issue of great importance raised by him.

Another point that I liked a lot, however I make the exception that it could have been worked on a little more, is the observation regarding the gender issue, in which he mentions that most of the data in the legal literature refer to men in delinquency, not focusing on women in this situation.

v. Background and solutions

In the background topic, the author explained once again the steps followed in the study, and explained some important points, which brought fluidity to the reading.

Extremely pertinent analysis when relating the majority black prison population with those incarcerated under apartheid, in South Africa, and in detriment of the number of white incarcerated, demonstrating a visible structural racism that permeates in the American prison system, as a reflection of a racism that permeates in socioeconomic structures and often privileges some races in detriment of others.

I also see a great point about the effects of intergenerational incarceration, where a country of young black men have been incarcerated, as another barrier to reintegration into post-prison life, which makes these young men face not only economic issues, but also the effects of their parents' behaviors in society.

I want to give special attention to the second case because it is a close friend of the author, brings a humanity that provokes the reader to empathize and puts him/her in the place of thought, where putting oneself in the place of the author, could happen to any African-American person that the reader knows and may have affection for. Important to spark attention and thought in the reader. Even more so for being arrested for drugs near school, something that is relatively common in today's society (which won't be the severity of the act), being that he didn't hurt anyone and was tricked into trying to help someone and caught at that time. The argument makes one think that it could happen to anyone and question how error-prone the judicial system is.

It could also raise a common problem in the United States, which is the privatization of prisons and the way in which the suffering of these young people is commodified, and the racial cut, in which the more people are incarcerated, the more the privatized prisons profit, which also causes an increase in the incarceration of black people, because they are the most vulnerable population.

As for the solutions, I believe they are concise and clear, demonstrating the author's knowledge and deep legal foundation, which does not make use of simplistic and populist solutions.

I only point out that more urgent solutions could have been cited, such as, for example, investment in public education policies and the economic empowerment of minority classes like those studied.

About the notes concerning the translation from English to French, it brought a cultured and objective language, which allows the reader to absorb the essence of what was studied by the author, even though there are some changes in writing and vocabulary in relation to the original project written in English.

Peer Review Report of Attorney Camille Molina-Brusley

The manuscript titled Etymological Injustice: *Formerly-Incarcerated* Youth with *Sociophysiological Challenges* examines the reintegration issues encountered by youth formerly imprisoned falling into two distinct categories: young people with disabilities and who are African-American.

Importantly, and uniquely, this book presents a valuable linguistic advantage as it was written in English and French, allowing for the carrying out of an evaluation relative to its content, firstly (1), as well as with respect to the quality of its translation from English to French, secondly (2).

This book focuses on an important matter in an innovative way and this topic seems to have received marginal scholarly and doctrinal treatment and should therefore be highly appreciated in this respect. More importantly, the topic addressed in this book is particularly interesting because it can significantly impact legal scholarship and the legal world, in calling for indispensable legal reforms in American society.

The topic of the reentry of young people, in general, is essential in a society that values protecting its members and the rule of law.

This type of research is, therefore, absolutely essential. Not only does it bring to light the importance of constantly improving penal reintegration policies, but it also focuses on two newly studied subgroups. Those two groups, although overrepresented in detention populations and possessing reintegration needs, are underrepresented in terms of academic interest and practical solutions tailored to their particular needs.

However, although this topic is exciting, the study carried out as part of this book reflects imperfections, in terms of the sufficiency of the solutions offered, and could have been refined along two veins: (a) regarding the structure and logic of certain arguments offered, and (b) regarding the scope in which the author explores the subject.

In presenting the subject and the stakes, the first part of the study does not allow for a justification of certain choices of the author, whereas these explanations would be, in my opinion, essential for a complete analysis. Mainly, I took interest in the two sub-groups chosen by the author, namely young people with a form of disability, and young African-Americans. Besides the fact that these two subgroups are overrepresented within the American penal and carceral system, and an obvious interest of the author in these groups, the book does not allow for a presentation of a sufficient explanation or justification for the choice of study of these two groups. Why study these two groups in particular? And why exclude Amerindians from the study, for example, when they are also overrepresented?

As a matter of fact, the two subgroups have totally different situations, and since their situations do not overlap, their studies cannot be compared. Studying the two sub-groups is fundamentally different in the reasons for the over-representation of each sub-group, the conditions of detention, the obstacles faced to reintegrating society, the potential solutions, and the proposed reforms.

This criticism might seem trivial however, it affects the document's structure. Another structural flaw is the problem of redundant data being presented. As an example, three different sections within the manuscript deal with the numbers of overrepresentation of the African American group, and they are (1) Pages 7 to 9 in the introductory section, "Numerical Scope of the Youth Affected," entirely focused on this topic; (2) Pages 21 and 22 in the section "Building Conceptual Connections: Mandela, U.S. Mass Incarceration, and the Juvenile Incarceration Debate;" and (3) Pages 28 and 30 in the section "Analyzing Black Youth and their Incarceration Journeys."

This last section, which is located in the middle of the manuscript, is entirely dedicated to the numbers of overrepresentation, again, whereas this data had been dealt with in the book's introduction.

Another important structural point is the book's methodological divergence from the doctrinal approach to conducting legal analysis. The author explains in the section "Breaking with Conventional and Myopic Legal Scholarship" his methodology, which manifestly breaks with the traditional approach of "doctrinal analysis" and rather focuses on "problems that laws have failed to solve" (see p. 12).

This approach could be valid but is not, in my opinion, sufficiently justified here. Firstly, a purely factual study would be okay if the manuscript really took interest in the problems of reintegration encountered by the two subgroups and then explained the solutions and proposed reforms linked to those problems.

Secondly, to know if, indeed, the laws cannot solve the problems raised, it's necessary to look into these laws. Excluding the study altogether makes the book's analysis incomplete.

A more complete and ideal study should, at least, take interest in the following points:

- How can - or cannot - reintegration laws in effect in the United States apply to the two sub-groups under study?
- Why are these laws lacking in relation to the specificities of the two groups studied?
- What societal problems can these laws not address?
- And therefore, what solutions and reforms are proposed to remedy these issues?

The second main problem encountered is that the book fails to remain strictly within the scope of the subject.

The book's first part (see II. and III.) sets out very lengthily and very clearly the stakes of the issues dealt with, the author's motivation, the research methods used, the approach adopted, and the definitions of the terms covered in the book. The subject is thus clearly explained: the reintegration of young people from the two subgroups studied.

However, a smaller proportion of the book appears to deal with reintegration. Two examples can be cited. The first one is that of the section "Building Conceptual Connections: Mandela,

U.S. Mass Incarceration, and the Juvenile Incarceration Debate" (see p. 21 and 22), which presents two fundamental problems: (i) a series of ideas marginally pushing forward the argument, and (ii) being somewhat tangential to the subject of youth reintegration. Although its title refers to the incarceration of minors, this point is not sufficiently dealt with in this section.

It is noted here that this section is not, per se, criticized on the basis of its content. These are, in absolute terms, important considerations, and all points made could give rise to very long and passionate debates. However, some considerations have absolutely no place in some parts of the book, or at the very least, the author fails to justify their interest and relevance.

The second example will be that of the case study n° 1: "The Blade Reese Case" (see p. 26 to 29). This case covers for three pages the story of Blade Reese, a young autistic man sentenced to thirty years and detained "as an adult" in the state of Indiana. If this story is fundamentally very interesting and could have been fascinating in another context, it has no direct link with the subject treated. Blade's handicap, hardly mentioned, is never presented as a factor of delinquency, nor as an obstacle to his reintegration, but only as a challenge during his prison time, which doesn't get at the heart of the book. Blade's case seems less relevant since this young man is still incarcerated and, a fortiori (with greater reason), will have to reintegrate into society as an adult.

On the other hand, the manuscript is missing some important points, or, at the very least, fails to justify why they are not addressed. Some examples include:

- Why are young people with disabilities overrepresented in the American penal system?
- What are some of the applicable reintegration laws?
- What are the current reintegration policies for young

people?

- What are the “transitional programs for juvenile delinquent youth” mentioned? Why are they not suitable for young people from both subgroups?

In conclusion, despite a very interesting subject and many good ideas, the book could have been further refined in multiple aspects.

Regarding the French version of the article, it is, overall, an excellent translation. The terms used are correct, the book’s language is formal, as well as its grammar and syntax are good. There are a few imprecisions, and some expressions seem to have been translated too literally, but this is in no way detrimental to understanding or reading the manuscript.

However, it seems important to mention that literal translation of certain expressions, when relating to notions that are well defined in law, can be detrimental to the reader’s comprehension. To cite an example, the expression “black letter law” has been literally translated as “loi de lettres noires”, which, literally in French, does not refer to any particular legal concept. The expression “règles de droit immuable” or “grands principes du droit” should have been preferred to refer to the same principle in American law. Another example could have been regarding the expression “strain theory” literally translated as “théorie de la souche” to which the more widely accepted expression “théorie de tension” is preferable.

Moreover, regarding another very specific point, the notion of “blackness” has been translated by the French expression “négritude”. I draw attention to the fact that this French term must be used with great caution, not referring to the same thing as in English. This term, very scarcely used, refers exclusively to a literary movement. Therefore, the use of this term is justified when the author mentions the literary current of Aimé Césaire and Paulette Narval, but in no case when he seeks to define the notion of "blackness" and Afro-American.

Apart from these few points, the translation is globally very satisfactory.

Camille Molina-Brusley is a practicing attorney. She was admitted to the Paris Bar in May of 2016 (nearly 7 years ago), has practiced law in Paris, and worked as a paralegal in New York. Educationally, Ms. Molina-Brusley graduated from the Paris Bar School in 2015, after completing the School's professional training program. In addition, Attorney Molina-Brusley graduated from the Sorbonne Law School, where she completed a master's degree in international criminal law (with honors) in 2011. Before, Sorbonne, Molina-Brusley was at the University of Kent, whence she obtained an English Law Diploma (with merit) in 2010. Before Kent, Camille attended Sorbonne Law School, whence she graduated with a bachelor's degree in law (with honors) in 2009. Attorney Molina-Brusley, a native French speaker who is also fluent in English and Spanish, performed a double-blind review of this book, *Etymological Injustice.*

This page left blank intentionally

Peer Review Report of Attorney Liisa Helmi Paultre

This review was written without knowledge of the author's identity by Liisa Helmi Paultre, a French lawyer and translator with a master's degree from the Sorbonne University in Paris with a double major in Law and Political Science. The author of this review has worked as a legal advisor and translator for 10 years, mainly in the media and entertainment industry, and has a long history of volunteering for several non-governmental organizations. The author of this review was born and raised in France and has a very good knowledge of French culture and language.

The book examines the challenges young African Americans face when re-entering general society after incarceration.

The Introduction starts with a powerful quote by Nelson Mandela: "There can be no keener revelation of a society's soul than the way it treats its children.". This quote is impactful as it appeals to everyone on a near-spiritual level.

In this introduction, the accent is on the author's personal involvement with people with sociophysical challenges. It sets the tone for the rest of the book, by communicating to the reader a strong sense of urgency.

The author's choice to use the first-person singular is impactful, as it creates an instant, almost personal, bond between the reader and the author.

The author's passion is effectively transmitted to the reader in this introduction and throughout the manuscript. The tone is sometimes accusatory, but it is always proportional to the gravity of the problem the author is describing.

The Methodology section is straightforward and provides a strong, fact-based background to the issues raised by the author. The author sets forth statistics reinforcing the author's choice to study a certain category of people, young African Americans with sociophysiological challenges.

The author emphasizes yet again the importance of giving former prisoners a chance to redeem themselves and to re-integrate them into our society. The author sometimes uses patriotic arguments, in line with the introductory Nelson Mandala quote about how the treatment of children says a lot about the dignity of a nation. The author uses American national identity and pride as a way to further implicate the reader, e.g. "who we are as a nation" (p.10). Whilst this argument could be effective on American readers, it will in all probability have a lesser impact on French readers. National identity and pride are in fact much less predominant in France. Therefore, French readers may find these arguments a bit chauvinistic. Furthermore, the author's choice to use "us" (translated as "nous") when talking about United States citizens could maybe be reconsidered, as French readers will most likely not identity to this common identity between the reader and the author.

In the Literature Review, the author, using doctrinal classifications, lays out the definition of the two key elements of his thesis: what it means to have sociophysiological challenges and what it means to be African American. The definition of sociophysiological challenges is particularly helpful, as it's not a common concept. The author's choice to use the term "sociophysiological challenges" instead of "disability" is more inclusive and seems logical considering the variety of challenges faced by formerly incarcerated people. Unfortunately, the term "etymological injustice", used in the title of the book, is not defined anywhere in the book.

Citing solid sources, the author mentions the link between sociophysiological challenges and gender, as young men with sociophysiological challenges are more bullied than women with sociophysiological challenges. This is relevant because substantially more young men are incarcerated than women, something that the author will further develop in his work.

The definition of blackness is perhaps a bit brief, although the author manages to demonstrate how "black" and "African American" are problematic umbrella terms. Even if the author is critical of the terms, they are still used throughout his text, maybe for lack of a better term.

However, the author makes sure to refer to other scholars who have studied the limitations of this categorization.

The Literature Review section is concluded by an enumeration of the literature's four biggest flaws in an agile manner, albeit he could have cited more examples and sources for each flaw. This enumeration is effective in underlining the importance and singularity of the author's work. The author is disagreeing with a lot of the current academic approaches to criminology, such as blaming criminality on personal characteristics and lack of morality.

Nelson Mandala is yet again used as a reference in the Background section, creating a common thread and making it easier for the reader to gain perspective on the issue raised by the author. Nelson Mandela is, indeed, overwhelmingly perceived as a hero throughout the world and his treatment in prison has been widely criticized. The parallel made by the author between Nelson Mandela's incarceration and the incarceration of African Americans in the United States is extremely poignant.

The accent is on the deep-rooted issues and intersecting factors leading to so many young African American being incarcerated and having difficulties re-entering society. The author chooses the "from the bottom up" approach supported by Richard Trembley, hence the importance to break the intergenerational cycle of incarceration by starting with the youth. The Blade Reese Case is used as a case study to further illustrate his point. The author highlights the lack of equipment and the harsh quality of life of the inmates of the Wabash Valley Correctional Facility with elaborate details. The case study skillfully finds a way to capture a glimpse of what it could feel like to be incarcerated for as long as Blade Reese has been, and the reader cannot help but feel empathy for him.

The emphasis is further made on the mass incarceration of Hispanics and African Americans, with statistics to support this huge disparity. At this point of the manuscript, the author has found his rhythm, constantly backing his arguments with hard facts and numbers, and always insisting on the systemic causes of the issues raised.

The second case study is the Harry Saintil Case, a drug-related first offense that sentenced a 17-year-old to 5 years of prison. This case study is very interesting as it tells the story of a man who tried his best to re-enter society, but ultimately took his own life after having faced too many obstacles and traumas as a result of his incarceration. As the author puts it "While statistics can be used to make generalizations and persuade, stories have a unique aspect—in the sense that they are more memorable". It is rare to have the author be so transparent about the tools he is using to convince his readers, and one can only applaud his honesty. He even addresses his readers directly, pushing them to not only focus on the statistics but to also remember the "human" element. The dramatic consequences of an ill-managed incarceration system are carefully highlighted in this section.

In the fifth section, the author addresses the Barriers to Re-Integration, starting by analyzing the common barriers to the specific barriers faced by youth with sociophysiological challenges, and, finally, by African American youth.

The author intentionally chooses not to further develop well-known common barriers, and, instead, focuses on the specific issues faced by young African Americans.

The enumeration of challenges faced by formerly incarcerated youth after they are released from prison makes his point clear: formerly incarcerated young African Americans continue to be punished even after they have served their sentence and are not given a fair chance to redeem themselves.

The author first focuses on the challenged youth's access to special education as a focal point, and he denounces the lack of relevance of the current criteria to access special education programs. The fact that students with disabilities lose their designations if they "achieve a satisfactory score on a state proficiency test or meet certain standards in their individualized education plans" pinpoints the absurdity of the system.

The author makes a valid assessment of how the misidentification of youth with sociophysiological challenges has consequences on the way we track and study the re-entry of formerly incarcerated youth.

The author then analyzes the specific barriers for African American youth, first by looking at the intergenerational incarceration of African Americans, a point he had introduced previously, and, secondly, by looking at the cultural and racial factors. The reader is guided through the deep roots of the problem. The author uses sociology and history to identify the systemic causes of the issue. The cultural aspect is a sensitive topic and is usually difficult to navigate, but the author manages to explore that aspect without shifting the blame on African Americans and their culture.

The manuscript's last section, which is also the lengthiest, is all about proposing concrete Solutions to the problems described previously, focusing on the social and professional reintegration of formerly incarcerated youth.

This section is extremely important as it brings hope for change. The previous sections were all about exposing all the issues and challenges faced by formerly incarcerated youth, and the extent of the issue can sometimes feel somewhat overwhelming to the reader.

The author lists all possible solutions, from professional skills training to prevent the sharing of juvenile records with the general public. The author makes an excellent job of finding systemic and pragmatic solutions to a complex, deep-rooted issue.

Emphasis is placed on racial awareness and identity development, using the examples of three francophone writers/poets: Aimé Césaire, Léon Damas, and Paulette Nardal. These examples are specifically interesting to French readers, considering empowering black identity is not as common in France. Race is still very taboo in France, and ethnic statistics are prohibited by the law, contrary to the United States. It is not usual for French scholars to encourage racial identity development, although it is becoming more and more talked about.

The author cites applicable laws and why – and how - they should be amended. A solution to the lack of funding is proposed by making rehabilitation more cost-effective, instead of simply demanding increased state funding.

His experience volunteering for Access Living seems to give him useful insight into what already available solutions urgently need to be reinforced.

Overall, this section is the most well-grounded and convincing part of the book. The proposed solutions all seem logical and effective in comparison to the flawed system in place. The author does not only criticize and tell us what needs to be changed and why – he also has solid propositions on how they can be changed. He proposes concrete changes that urgently need to be made, whilst always finding the means to materialize such changes.

The Conclusion emphasizes the variety of the needs of juvenile prisoners, especially those with sociophysiological challenges, and how the current "default" path is not adapted to them. The author re-traces the doctrine and literature on the subject, and the facts and statistics backing up their assessment. The Conclusion sometimes fails to summarize and recollect the author's arguments, methodology, and plan of action being laid out in broad terms at the end of the Conclusion.

The language is for the most part fluid and easy to read in both French and English versions. The author makes a bold choice to be very direct and transparent about his approach, which creates a sort of trust between the reader and the author. The content has been skillfully adapted in the French translation, and you can feel that the author adjusted his thesis in a tailor-made, thoughtful way. However, a few legal translations are a bit imprecise, e.g. "lines of cases" (p.11) is incorrectly translated as "lignes d'affaires". Furthermore, some arguments, such as appealing to the national identity and pride of American readers, should maybe be further adapted to the French audience.

Overall, the author makes poignant arguments and by the end of the manuscript, the reader is convinced of the urgency to reform the United States juvenile delinquency system. The author's sources are strong and always relevant to the point being made. The author's passion for his subject is contagious, and skillfully manages to couple fact-based arguments with human elements, therefore appealing to both the reader's rationality and empathy. The solutions he is proposing seem reasonable and urgent to implement.

Peer Review Report of Attorney Natalia Benlloch (alias: Natalia Benlloch Moya)

I hereby present myself as the author of this blind review. I am Natalia Benlloch, a jurist specialized on International Human Rights Law. I am a law school graduate by the University of Valencia (Spain), and I hold an LLM on International Law and Human Rights by the University of Maastricht (The Netherlands). My attendance to the Summer School on International Human Rights Law at the European University Institute (EUI) in Florence also contributed to my educational background. Moreover, I also participated in the International Humanitarian Law course provided by the International Committee of the Red Cross (ICRC). I also took isolated courses on the International Law Masters at the Université Libre de Bruxelles (ULB). My professional experience has been mostly shaped by working in local law firms in Valencia (Spain) and an NGO in Brussels (Belgium). But certainly my most enriching experience was working at Latham & Watkins LLP, where my work focused on Pro Bono opportunities and on Mergers & Acquisition procedures before the European Commission in Brussels.

Currently I cooperate with humanitarian projects in South America. At the moment I am supporting a foundation that offers help to women victims of sexual exploitation in the city of El Alto in Bolivia.

i. Introduction

The *Etymological Injustice* manuscript brilliantly and sensitively exposes the hurdles faced by Afro-American and sociophysiological challenged youth within the US imprisonment system and the difficulties of their reintegration. Throughout the book, the author reveals a biased and inconsistent US system that clearly fails to protect and guarantee fundamental rights to these youth groups. Overall, the author's input in the topic and the data collection work he conducted, on which he relies to develop his arguments, are undeniably unique and strong. In a very original manner by combining his personal experience and academic skills, the author addresses issues that should be more on the spotlight. Both versions, the English and French one, display a serious academic level and thorough research skills. That is why I will support the publication of the present book throughout my review.

I have organized my paper following the structure of the manuscript. I will present and defend my arguments in favour of the present book highlighting the strengths of each section. I will also contribute with certain suggestions to the author to further enhance his work.

ii. Introduction of the Manuscript

In the introduction the author already reveals the human and touching approach that he will display throughout his book. He enlightens the reader with the original relation between the experience of Nelson Mandela in prison and the United States incarceration system.

I would only suggest to guide the reader by including a description of the manuscript's structure, where the author names the topics that he will address.

iii. Methodology

Throughout this section, the author does an excellent job at stating the importance of the research and the gravity of the situation for the Afro-American youth and those suffering from sociophysiological conditions who have been incarcerated.

While from a jurist perspective I would have enjoyed a different opinion about a doctrinal analysis, I do understand and value the perspective that unfortunately the law may fail to protect by not taking into account the social context.

iv. Literature Review

This section plays a strong role within this book, since it allows the reader to be familiarised with the essential and controversial concepts of "disability" and "blackness". The reader can appreciate the passion that lies between the lines and his genuine interest in the topic.

I would have certainly enjoyed to read more about the debate on the inappropriateness and poor use of the terms "black" and "Afro-American" in the United States. While I also understand that these are debates to be sparked and developed in a hopefully near future.

Nevertheless, I would advise to not translate these terms into French to ensure the reasoning of the author's arguments.

v. Background

The author's research skills are undoubtedly evidenced in this section. In a very direct and concise way, he makes the reader understand the consequences of a weak incarceration system that lacks resources in the United States. He provides concerning rates on black men incarceration and concisely explains some of the root factors that lead youth to end up as imprisoned criminals. It undoubtedly casts doubt on a system, which remains racist and unfair and whose direct victims are a collective of vulnerable young people in need of stability, attention and support.

The strength of this section is given by the two case studies that the author brings as part of his personal experience, where he evidences the appalling consequences of the system. While I was very pleased reading this section, I realized that the author changes his writing register significantly in the case studies description. He moves from a formal and academic tone to a novel descriptive register, which can also be perceived in the French translation.

vi. Barriers to Re-Integration

The author's thorough research skills continue to be displayed in this section. He explores and evidences the flaws of a system that hampers youth with sociophysiological challenges and Afro-Americans to reintegrate into society. He provides a challenging panorama of what these young people have to endure after leaving prison. This section deepens in the difficulties, and even some times impossibility, of youth to receive an adequate education and the administrative hurdles that have such a determining impact in their lives.

I find absolutely strong and groundbreaking the author's view and explanation of the Afro-American youth struggles to reconnect with their own culture, and to embrace the feeling of belonging. I find brilliant how the author denounces the mainstream of African-American culture in the US, which is not rooted in a genuine interest, but it is more perceived as a shallow "fashion".

I believe the reader would appreciate a deeper insight on the consequences and mental health problems of Afro-American youth due to previous parental incarceration. I find this topic utterly relevant and not sufficiently explored yet.

vii. Solutions

The solutions provided by the author are clearly influenced by his personal experience in the organization Access Living. The latter has undoubtedly provided him with a pragmatic view of the roots of the problems faced by youth. This understanding of the problem is reflected throughout the manuscript and consequently it naturally raises the quality of the text. For instance, I was very pleased to read some of his solutions inspired by French artistic movements.

viii. Easing Youth Transitions Through Legal Reforms Avenued

As a jurist I was very pleased to read the legal reforms proposed in this final section, where the author also succeeds in shedding light on the law inconsistency in protecting Afro–American youth and those suffering from sociophysiological challenges. The list of legal reforms proposed by the author follow a very logic and thorough approach. They are thought to reinforce those areas of the law that lack an enforcement mechanism and that suffer from legal loopholes.

ix. Conclusion

The author has thoroughly responded along the manuscript to all the questions presented in the introduction. Hence the conclusion should be used to summarize his view and stress the reasoning achieved throughout his work, avoiding to introduce new information. To ensure that the conclusion meets the quality revealed for the above work, I would enjoy reading a last strong statement that leaves the reader with the feeling that it was worth reading the author and his work.

In essence, the author has contributed to this topic with a new perspective and a thorough and detailed research based on an outstanding data collection. As such, I believe this manuscript qualifies for publication, in the hope that it will get the attention of many more.

ACKNOWLEDGMENTS

Concerning this book, as well as beyond, I would like to acknowledge the following individuals:

Sheila Bedi, JD,

Peter Cannavo, PhD,

Monica Llorente, JD,

J. Samuel Tenenbaum, JD, and

Nigel Westmaas, PhD.

This page left blank intentionally

ABOUT THE AUTHOR

Woodger Faugas, JD, Esq., is a researcher and licensed attorney. He graduated with senior research honors from Northwestern University Pritzker School of Law, with a Juris Doctor (JD) degree. He also graduated from Hamilton College, magna cum laude and Phi Beta Kappa, with a World Politics degree. After working in law, education, and management, Woodger is now pursuing a Medicinae Doctor (MD) degree at the University of California, San Francisco, (UCSF) School of Medicine.

www.ingramcontent.com/pod-product-compliance
Ingram Content Group UK Ltd.
Pitfield, Milton Keynes, MK11 3LW, UK
UKHW061545051026
15625UKWH00021B/688/J
* 9 7 9 8 9 8 7 5 5 6 6 0 3 *